value added tax

A report by the National Economic Development Office

ALAN R. WOODS
6, BROXBOURNE CLOSE,
CHERRY HINTON,
CAMBRIDGE.

GW00630677

London
Her Majesty's Stationery Office 1971

The National Economic Development Office is an independent body, publicly financed, which represents the three parties involved in industrial and economic development— management, trade unions, and government. This publication has been prepared by NEDO *which is solely responsible for its contents. For administrative convenience the booklet is printed and published through Her Majesty's Stationery Office.*

First published August 1969
Second edition April 1971

National Economic
Development Office
Millbank Tower
Millbank London sw1
01–834 3811
April 1971

SBN 11 700550 9

Contents

Foreword by
Sir Frederick Catherwood,
Director general of NEDO

1 Since it was set up in 1962 the National Economic Development Council has been interested in the effects of taxation on economic growth, and in particular in the possibility that a value added tax of the kind already adopted widely in Europe would have a contribution to make in any major reform of the British system of taxation. In the 'Orange Book' publication of 1963, *Conditions Favourable to Faster Growth*, attention was drawn to the contribution which a VAT might make to growth in certain circumstances. Then in the summer of 1966 the Council again turned its attention to the question and, following a discussion in June of that year, invited me to set up a committee to examine the implications of a value added tax in the United Kingdom and to report back.

2 The committee included representatives from the CBI, the TUC, and the National Economic Development Office, and it has also been able to draw on the advice and experience of a number of consultants, both academic and industrial. I would particularly like to mention the contribution made to the committee's work by Mr A Aylmer, of Unilever, Mr L J E Beeson of the Birmingham Small Arms Co Ltd, and Mr C T H Plant of the Inland Revenue Staff Federation who gave a great deal of time and effort to our discussions. We have also benefited considerably from the advice and assistance of Mr David Stout of University College, Oxford (now seconded to the National Economic Development Office as its Economic Director). The committee was also helped in many ways by departmental officials from HM Customs and Excise, the Inland Revenue, HM Treasury, the Department of Economic Affairs, the Central Statistical Office, and also from various Embassies in London, none of whom, however, is in any way committed to any of the views which are expressed in this report. Altogether the committee held some sixteen meetings between October 1966 and October 1968, and considered various economic and social aspects of value added taxation. It also conducted a detailed survey of industrial views through about twenty of the Economic Development Committees. Visits were paid to four European countries (Denmark, France, Germany and the Netherlands) to discuss some of the problems of value added taxation as they had appeared in practice in these countries. In the course of these visits talks were held with government officials, businessmen and trade unionists and we would very much wish to express our gratitude to them for their help, for their hospitality, and for the trouble they took to provide us with the information which we sought. The practical experience of these countries in operating a VAT under very diverse conditions (not all of which of course are relevant to the UK) has been immensely helpful. It has enabled us to see the advantages and the disadvantages of the system in a context of reality rather than of theory or hypothesis alone.

3 My purely personal view about the VAT is that, given the right conditions, which are spelled out in this report, it could enable improvements to be made in our fiscal system which could increase economic efficiency and

help the balance of payments. Moreover, this could be accomplished without regressive or significantly inflationary effects. However, I fully recognise that the tax would raise formidable problems of administration (for both industry and government) and, in so far as it involves a degree of self assessment, of tax morality also. Moreover, major tax changes, even when they are considered desirable, cannot be introduced at too frequent intervals, and European experience suggests that the introduction of a VAT in this country would require at least two or three years' preparatory work.

4 As this second edition goes to press the Chancellor has just announced that he proposes to abolish both purchase tax and SET in April 1973 and introduce, in their place, a broadly-based VAT, with relief for food, books, newspapers and periodicals and small businesses, of the form we have broadly described and analysed in this report. Two years is a short time for all of us to prepare ourselves for this major restructuring of our taxation system. I hope that this report will help by answering some of the questions that will arise and reminding us of what work there is still to be done.

Introduction, summary and conclusions

1.1 A value added tax (hereinafter called simply a VAT) in recent years has come to occupy a central position in discussions of taxation in Britain. There are a number of reasons for this. First of all, there has been the possibility that this country would one day become a member of the EEC, in which case the question would arise of adopting the common system of tax on value added as set out in the Directives of the EEC Commission. Secondly, it has been widely claimed that this form of tax has certain positive economic benefits, or at least avoids certain economic drawbacks, as compared with other taxes. Thirdly, there is a perennial feeling that there is a need for 'tax reform', and it has been argued that, because of its comprehensive and far reaching character, the adoption of a VAT would make possible and, indeed, inevitable a fundamental reshaping of the tax system.

1.2 One of the difficulties which has been encountered in writing this report has been the need to distinguish between the general case, if it exists, for a change in taxation methods, and the particular form of change which would be implied by the adoption of a VAT. Thus many of both the merits and the demerits which a VAT possesses are shared by other taxes. For example, it is not exclusively an advantage of a VAT that it would broaden the base of indirect taxation, for this, if it were desired, could be achieved in several other ways. Nor is it exclusively a criticism of VAT that there are likely to be complications in its administration, for other taxes have been criticised on this score. The possible introduction of a VAT should therefore be seen as a special case within a much broader set of fiscal considerations.

1.3 It is clear from much popular comment that there is a good deal of misunderstanding about the essential nature of a VAT. These misunderstandings range from the cruder views that it is in some sense a means of subsidising exports, or that it contributes to efficiency by taxing costs, to doubts as to what transactions would or would not be liable to pay the tax or yield tax credits. It is also important to remember that *a VAT is a tax;* it is not that fiscal philosopher's stone, a subsidy which yields revenue.

1.4 Chapter 2 of the report aims to set out the general principles of the working of the value added tax in such a way that at least some of these basic issues can be clarified. It shows, most importantly, that a VAT is essentially a tax which falls on consumer spending, but which is collected in instalments in the course of production and distribution in proportion to the value added at each stage in the process. (Purchase tax is also a tax which falls on consumer spending but which is collected at an earlier stage, ie wholesale, on the basis of the value of the article at that stage.) So that the tax will *not* fall on costs (and this is its great merit,) any tax paid by a producer (in the tax-inclusive price of his purchases) may be offset as a claim against the tax liability on his sales. Thus, the manufacturer of a component pays, to the Government, the tax due on his sale, recovers it by passing it on in the price to his customer who in turn can then count it as a credit against the subsequent tax liability on his sales. The Government gets the revenue in instalments as goods pass through the productive and distributive process; the tax is paid by the sellers and credited to the purchasers until the process ends with the final consumer who bears the accumulated tax in the final selling price but cannot himself claim a credit. This last point is an important one, because it reveals that unless a person is liable to pay VAT on his sales, he cannot claim *credits* for the tax element in his purchases. This is evident in the case of the final consumer, but it is often forgotten by other groups who think it would be in their interests to claim exemption from the tax, without realising that by doing so they could debar themselves from obtaining tax credits on their purchases.

1.5 VAT does not arise on export sales, although any tax paid on goods or services entering into exports can be credited to the exporter in the usual way. At present there is some overspill of indirect taxes into exports: a small amount of purchase tax, e g on office stationery and company cars, falls incidentally on industrial costs, and so too do duties on fuel oil, for example. If these taxes were replaced by a VAT which could be rebated this overspill would be avoided; if all else remained unchanged costs would be lowered by that amount and exports would thus be made more competitive. (It is technically possible to modify the machinery of purchase tax to avoid the overspill on industrial costs, but for revenue reasons this has not so far been done. Alternatively this overspill could of course be rebated in some other way if this were desired, as was attempted when the export rebate was in force). Equally, if a direct tax such as corporation tax is reflected in costs, and if this were replaced by a VAT (or indeed any rebatable tax) then a similar effect would occur. In other words, it is not the imposition of a VAT which might help exports, in this respect it is neutral like purchase tax, but the removal of other currently non-rebatable taxes which a VAT might make possible.

1.6 Chapter 3 deals with the present structure of UK taxation. It suggests that while the overall burden of taxation on the British economy is not high by international standards, the way in which it is distributed between different groups of taxpayers helps to foster this impression. A VAT is, however, still a tax and its introduction would not necessarily make this country any more lightly or heavily taxed than it is now; what it could do if desired would be to contribute to shifting the burden of taxes either from earnings to spending, or as between one form of spending and another. In other words the introduction of a VAT at appropriate rates, because of its comprehensiveness and revenue raising potential, offers an opportunity for a major exercise in tax switching.

1.7 Any area of UK taxation would be eligible for consideration in a switch of this kind. The choice is one which would be primarily determined by social and political considerations. Thus, personal income tax might be reduced, either on general incentive grounds, or in order to compensate for some of the income effects resulting from the price changes brought about by the VAT. Alternatively, corporate taxation might be reduced to derive some of the benefits to efficiency and the balance of payments which have been argued.

1.8　Indirect taxes already provide a high proportion of total tax revenue (it is a popular fiscal myth that we do not rely on taxes on expenditure to the same extent as other countries), but a very high proportion of it is derived from an extremely narrow base of expenditure on tobacco, drink and hydrocarbon oils. Moreover, even although purchase tax is more widely spread, the greater part of its revenue, on its present coverage, comes from a limited range of highly taxed consumer durables.

1.9　Our present fiscal system, like that of other countries, is not designed simply to provide the Government with funds to pay for its expenditure. It is used as an instrument of economic policy and demand management, and of social policy. In the latter connection the principle of 'the ability to pay' has the effect of reducing the degree of pre-tax inequalities of income. Personal income tax and especially surtax contribute largely to this, and they are supplemented, in order to further reduce inequalities of pre-tax incomes, by a system of benefits and allowances. However, our indirect taxes, taken as a whole work in the opposite direction and tend to fall relatively more heavily on the lower income groups. All in all our taxes are only 'progressive' (i e tending to reduce pre-tax inequalities of income) at the highest levels, because of surtax; at the lowest levels, among old age pensioners, for example, they are quite regressive, because of the very high specific duties on beer and tobacco. Over a large middle band of incomes the total burden of taxation is broadly proportional to income. Such progressiveness as there is in the totality of our fiscal arrangements comes largely from social benefits (pensions and family allowances) rather than from taxation, but given the various objects which taxes have to fulfil it is unlikely that any one fiscal device could achieve all of them simultaneously or equally.

1.10　Chapter 4 deals with various aspects of the VAT in the ten European countries which have adopted it or are in the process of doing so. It shows the wide variations which can exist even within the EEC, where the broad pattern of the tax has been laid down in the Commission's Directives, and the variations are even greater if the non-EEC countries are taken into account. These do not simply arise from differences in the levels of tax rates (which are wide), but from the number of rates and from their coverage as well as from the length of tax periods, arrangements for rebates, and other administrative considerations. Moreover, each country has its own special interests with respect to the treatment of particular industries or sectors, such as agriculture or small firms, and these have had to be accommodated by special arrangements within the broad framework of the VAT.

1.11 The main reason why the six countries of the Community adopted the common VAT system was the need to find a mutually acceptable method of indirect taxation which would operate without producing distortions in the flows of trade among the members of the economic union. The three Scandinavian countries do a large part of their trade with the EEC, and are indeed aspiring members of the Community, and this consideration undoubtedly carried some weight with them in reaching their decision. So far as the UK is concerned, already about 40 per cent of our trade is now with countries having, or proposing to have, a VAT. Therefore, whether we adopt the tax or not, in so far as it has any effect on exports and imports, it is of relevance to us.

1.12 The discussion in Chapter 4 of the way in which the tax operates in these countries is not merely descriptive, but it throws light on some of the detailed practical problems which can arise in the actual implementation of the tax (such as the various categories of exemptions, the treatment of stocks, and so on) and how they are being dealt with.

1.13 Chapters 2, 3 and 4 are largely concerned with setting the scene for a consideration of what might be the problems of a VAT in the UK, and what decisions would have to be taken in order to introduce it.

1.14 Naturally a primary concern of most people, certainly in their capacity as taxpayers, would be with the rates at which the new tax was levied. Here the most important considerations would be:

a The Government's revenue requirements at the time, having regard to what other taxes were being modified or replaced
b The coverage of goods and services subject to the various rates and/or exemptions.

What the actual rates might be in practice cannot be foreseen, but for illustrative purposes two possible schemes have been looked at: the first is a single rate of VAT of 10 per cent on all transactions except for foodstuffs, and the second would have a basic rate of 12½ per cent, a higher 'luxury' rate of 25 per cent, and a wider range of exemptions, also including foodstuffs. Each of these two schemes would yield revenue of around £1,500–1,700 million which is, by and large, the kind of order of magnitude which would be required to make the introduction of a VAT worthwhile. If purchase tax and SET were to be replaced, and the levels of existing excise duties adjusted so that the net yield from them was the same as now, the effect would be, if no offsetting reductions were made, to raise the cost of living index by about 2½ to 3 per cent. By exempting food in both cases the effect on the balance of income distribution, compared with present taxes, appears to be very small, and certainly the amount of revenue raised would be at least sufficient to make any necessary compensatory adjustments to other taxes or benefits.

1.15 There can be little doubt that the administrative problems presented by a VAT would be considerable, and indeed could well be the decisive factor in determining whether the tax would be adopted in this country. Compared with purchase tax, a VAT would involve a much greater number of traders being brought into the tax net, and virtually all their sales and purchase transactions being recorded for tax purposes. The greater the number of rates of tax, or the wider the range of exemptions, the greater would be the risk of anomalies and of increasing the complexity of the arrangements. It is difficult to be precise about this, but it has been estimated that several thousand additional tax officials would be required to administer a VAT in the UK. The total number required could vary widely around 6,000–8,000, depending on the complexity of the system adopted and the extent to which administrative practices and techniques might be modified. Evidence from the revenue authorities in this country and from the European countries have pointed to a gross figure of this order. There would also be an additional cost to industry in processing the data required for tax payments and rebates.

1.16 Perhaps the question which has occupied the central place in recent discussions of a VAT in this country has been the extent to which it could help the balance of payments and industrial efficiency. It has been said already, but it cannot be repeated too often, that in itself a VAT does not claim to yield these benefits; what is important are the consequential effects on costs and competitiveness of reductions in *other* taxes which a comprehensive VAT might make possible. In particular, attention has been focused on the possibility of a switch from corporation tax to VAT to achieve these ends. The Richardson Committee, which examined the case for a VAT as a substitute for profits tax in 1963 (Cmnd 2300), thought that there would be no benefits from such a switch because the introduction of a VAT would cause other costs and prices— including wages—to rise, thus offsetting any benefits (and these in any case are speculative) which might arise from the cut in profits tax. Although this is a very real danger this present report takes a somewhat different view. If a big enough cut in corporation tax were to be made, and if the rate of VAT were such as simply to replace the lost revenue, then the likelihood is that because of the sharper competitive climate which now exists, and the improvement in accounting methods (especially the greater attention to post-tax profit calculations), there would be benefits to the balance of payments and efficiency. However, in practical terms there are problems: first, at present the abolition of, or a really major cut in, corporation tax appears very unlikely, and a small reduction, or the avoidance of a small increase, would be unlikely to have a significant effect on costs and pricing decisions; secondly, if there were only a small cut in corporation tax it would not be worth introducing a VAT at a rate which only produced an equal yield to the revenue lost; but if the VAT rate were higher than this the risk of increasing costs would be enhanced; thirdly, there are other economic effects of corporation tax which might need to be compensated for.

In view of these facts it is, therefore, necessary to consider whether there are likely to be any advantages from other tax switches.

1.17 The possibility of substituting VAT for indirect taxes, such as purchase tax or SET, raises a different set of issues which are basically three in number. First, as has already been seen, our present indirect tax arrangements are (except for the SET) rather narrowly based on specific duties on drink, tobacco and hydrocarbon oils (though the incidence of the oils tax is widely spread), and differentiated ad valorem duties on, mainly, durable consumer goods. Apart from any implied social judgements as to the desirability of these forms of expenditure, the relevant considerations are:

a Whether these taxes are the best instruments to meet the revenue and other requirements having regard to the effect on the buoyancy of the revenue of high specific duties

b The possibly damaging effects on the economy of such a high degree of selectivity as compared with a more broadly based ad valorem system such as a VAT.

The second, related, considerations are the relative advantages and disadvantages of the two tax systems in acting as a regulator of economic activity. On the one hand, narrowly based specific duties offer the advantages of greater selectivity with the disadvantages of higher rates and the possibility of economic irrelevance or ineffectiveness resulting from the switching of expenditure. On the other hand, a VAT would probably be less selective, but in general would be likely to have lower rates and to provide less opportunity for diverting expenditure. Thirdly, under our existing indirect tax arrangements, some of these taxes spill over into industrial costs and prices. With a VAT there is a built-in mechanism for avoiding this, whereas under present arrangements special measures would be required which have not so far proved practicable.

1.18 Finally, Chapter 6 and the Appendix set out a range of industrial views and comments based on a questionnaire which was circulated by the National Economic Development Office through the Economic Development Committees (EDCs). These opinions, while valuable and informative, cannot be regarded in any full sense as 'the views of industry' about a VAT, for although the coverage of the EDCs was widespread in, predominantly, the private sector, it was nevertheless not comprehensive. Moreover, in order to keep the enquiry within manageable proportions the scope of the questionnaire was confined to a limited set of questions which it was hoped, however, would throw sufficient light on general attitudes to the tax to be of value. It should also be remembered, of course, that the EDCs are tripartite bodies with members drawn from government departments, trade unions and management interests. These three groups did not participate equally in all the EDCs; government representatives in particular felt it necessary to reserve their position in view of the nature of the problem, and, in general, the trade unions too reserved their position on the broader economic and social aspects of the question. Thus in most cases the views expressed, especially on questions relating to costs, prices, and so on, were primarily those of the management side, or of the trade association which primarily represents their interests.

1.19 On the whole the views expressed about the general desirability, or the specific effects, of a VAT were diverse and inconclusive, and there was no unanimity or even a general consensus either in favour of, or against, the introduction of the tax, or about its general industrial and economic impact. Also, the assumptions on which some of the conclusions were reached (for example, on the other tax changes which might be made, or on the levels at which a VAT might be imposed) varied very widely between one industry and another. However, it was clear that there is a very genuine and wide-spread concern in industry mainly about the complexity of our existing tax arrangements (both direct and indirect), and that at least a part of the intuitive appeal which a VAT seems to possess lies in the belief that it is capable of being simple and comprehensive and would enable much of the present tax jungle to be cleared away. This belief is not necessarily altogether well founded. Complexity in taxation often arises from a search for equity as between different groups of taxpayers, and it is something which could probably only be disposed of at a price which might not always be as acceptable in reality as it would seem to be in prospect. Nevertheless this is not to say that all the complications in our system can be explained in this way. At least some of them arise from the age of our tax system and the continued ad hoc accretions to it over the years. Some of the views of the EDCs clearly reflected special sectional interests: thus, certain industries whose products are highly taxed at present through purchase tax felt that their burden would be reduced if a more broadly based VAT were introduced, though this more often than not reflected the view that the *rate* of tax would be lower rather than that the VAT method of collection was desirable.

1.20 The balance of argument as to the effects on the balance of payments and efficiency of substituting a VAT for a part of direct taxation on companies, was that these effects would probably be favourable *provided that* the offsetting reduction in the direct taxes was large enough . If this could not be guaranteed, then the disadvantages of higher administrative costs and problems of income distribution would loom correspondingly larger and would tend to tip the balance the other way. It was quite clear that if a VAT were seen simply as an additional tax, and unless a very substantial modification of existing taxes—if not the total abolition of some of them—could be ensured, then it would not be welcomed.

1.21 It is not the purpose of this report to draw conclusions or to make recommendations about whether or not it would be desirable to introduce a VAT in this country. It aims to set out some of the main considerations which would be involved if a VAT *were* seriously to be considered as a possibility. Before this could happen one prior question would need to be answered: do we wish to increase the proportion of revenue raised by a broadly based, ad valorem tax on consumption, in preference to increasing direct taxation on individuals or companies, or to raising existing more narrowly based or specific indirect taxes? If the answer to this question is Yes, then a VAT takes its place alongside other possibilities such as a more comprehensive purchase tax, a general sales tax, or perhaps variants of a payroll tax and the SET.

1.22 The considerations which have to be taken into account in reaching any decision about the desirability of appropriateness of a VAT would need to include answers to a further series of questions:

a What to do about the services sector? It is desired that services should be taxed equally with goods, ie laundries as well as washing machines, hairdressers as well as hair driers, cinema performances as well as cine cameras? Purchase tax is not, as it stands, suitable for dealing with this, though SET achieves the same objective.

b What about retailing? This is related to the previous point, but in any consideration of a VAT the costs of including very large numbers of retailers would need to be set against the advantage of universality in the system.

c What to do about the problems of the spill-over of taxes into costs? This is not a serious problem at present, but it is one which was dealt with to some extent by the export rebate, which was widely held to be of value to industry, and to have been abandoned only because of international pressure; secondly it is a problem which is likely to grow greater rather than less, especially if the purchase tax was greatly extended to produce a comprehensive or nearly comprehensive tax on goods. In such a case the effective implementation of any offsetting measures which might be available would become essential.

1.23 So far as a VAT is concerned, it *would* automatically include the services sector, it *could* include retailing, and it *would* avoid the problem of spill-over. Against this would need to be set the *certainty* of its greater administrative complexity, the *probability* of a rise in prices, and the *possibility* of some regressive impact which would require correction.

General characteristics of value added tax 2

General description

2.1 Value added taxation is levied or is shortly to be levied in eight countries: Denmark, Sweden and the six members of the EEC. It is also under active consideration in Norway. In discussing the main features of a VAT the definition of 'value added' is the one generally employed in these countries.*

2.2 VAT is a method of taxing, by instalments, *final consumer spending in the domestic economy*. It is a multi-stage tax, rather than a single-stage one like purchase tax. Also, unlike purchase tax, VAT is, in principle, comprehensive: that is to say, instead of the tax being levied on a specific list of goods and services, it falls on all final consumer goods and services, except for goods and services which are explicitly exempted. Taxing on a value added basis ensures that each input into final consumer output is taxed once and once only, because tax paid on inputs at a previous stage in production may be rebated. This is in contrast to the gross turnover (sometimes called 'cascade') taxes which were common in Europe, under which the same elements of value added were taxed cumulatively, as goods passed along the production chain.

2.3 How is it that final *consumption* only is the base of the tax when in fact the tax is levied on sales of capital goods and consumer goods alike, and when one important input into final consumption is the depreciation of capital goods? VAT is certainly charged to, and is payable by, the producer and seller of capital goods, but is recovered in the form of a rebate or credit by the purchaser, who is himself liable to VAT on his sales. Capital services are thus only the subject of tax to the extent that they contribute to current final domestic consumption, for it is only at this last stage that the levying of VAT gives rise to no corresponding credit. New capital goods which do *not* increase the current period's domestic consumption (ie net additions to capital stock as distinct from depreciation) are not the subject of irrecoverable tax in the current period. Only as their services become by degrees incorporated in increases in *final consumer output* are the contributions of these investments the eventual subject of irrecoverable tax. This is a special case of the general principle of VAT: if an *input* has been taxed the taxable *output* base is correspondingly reduced. There is thus no double taxation such as would arise if both outputs and inputs were levied cumulatively.

2.4 How is it that only *domestic* consumption is taxed? Under a VAT régime, export turnover is not subject to taxation, but tax credits are allowed for the VAT element in all inputs purchased from other domestic suppliers or directly imported, whether destined to be embodied in taxed domestic sales or untaxed exports. If, upon the introduction of a VAT the prices of inputs

---

* For an exhaustive treatment of all the theoretical variations of VAT see Clara K Sullivan, 'The Tax on Value Added', Columbia UP, 1965. The EEC directives on VAT, and the practice and intentions of the nine countries referred to are described in the journal 'European Taxation', July/August 1967, Feb. 1968 and Nov./Dec. 1968 (published by the International Bureau of Fiscal Documentation, Amsterdam).

net of VAT invoiced remain unchanged, then the effect of those provisions is precisely to free exports entirely from the VAT*.

2.5 On the other hand, the whole of imports, at their cif value and including customs duties, is liable to the VAT automatically as the goods cross the border, or are drawn from bonded warehouses. Where these imports are not final imports but are inputs (such as machinery or materials) into the production of other goods or services, the VAT element in their price is deductible from the VAT payable by the user of these imports. Thus imports, too, are taxed once and once only, as they enter final domestic consumption.

2.6 The exclusion of export value added, and the inclusion of imports, in the value added tax base enshrines the 'country of destination' principle in this form of indirect taxation. This is the same principle that applies with purchase tax, except to the extent that some purchase tax may fall upon goods which eventually enter exports. A VAT may be contrasted, in this respect, with, say, the duty on hydrocarbon oils, which falls on inputs into domestic production of goods for home and export markets alike.

2.7 To illustrate this point, if tariff-free trade is carried on between two countries A and B, and A imposes only 'country of origin' taxes† (such as the UK's hydrocarbon oil duties), while B imposes only 'country of destination' taxes (such as a VAT), then A's exports to B are subject to two separate tax régimes (its own domestic duty and B's VAT), and B's exports to A are subject to neither. This of course was a major reason why it was necessary for the Common Market to harmonise its indirect taxation, in this case on the 'country of destination' basis.

Methods of imposing a VAT

2.8 It can be seen that the term 'value added' refers rather to the method of collection than to the eventual base of the tax, which is not what the economist understands by the term 'value added'. VAT is collected on the value of sales at each stage of production, but is recovered by the purchaser who is permitted to set the tax he has paid against the tax he himself is due to pay on his own sales. Only for the final purchaser of consumer goods and services in the home economy is there no recovery of tax passed on. This final purchaser is not himself liable to pay VAT, and so can claim no credit for tax invoiced and passed on to him.

* *If a VAT were introduced as part of some change in the tax structure which reduced the tax-exclusive prices of inputs into exports below what they would otherwise have been, or if such a change reduced the tax-exclusive prices of domestic substitutes for imports below what they would otherwise have been, then the change in the tax structure incorporating VAT would not be neutral so far as the balance of payments is concerned. This point is dealt with further in Chapter 5.*

† *Included in this term are taxes which fall on inputs into output regardless of whether the latter is destined for home consumption or foreign markets. Hydrocarbon oil duties are an example of such taxes.*

2.9 In Table 1, as a simple illustration of this process, we take the case of a domestic producer of primary products who sells them to a manufacturer who processes them, and in turn sells them to a wholesaler, who sells them to a retailer, who sells them to a consumer. A flat rate of VAT of 10 per cent is assumed on all transactions.

Table 1

Value added		(1) Purchase price to seller excluding VAT	(2) Purchase price including VAT	(3) Selling price excluding VAT	(4) VAT liability	(5) VAT credit	(6) VAT due
100	Primary producer sells to manufacturer	0	0	100	10	0	10
100	Manufacturer sells to wholesaler	100	110	200	20	10	10
50	Wholesaler sells to retailer	200	220	250	25	20	5
50	Retailer sells to consumer	250	275	300	30	25	5
300							

Total cost to consumer = 330, of which total VAT = 30

It will be noted that:

a Because each business actually pays tax (Col 6) only on the value it adds (not on the sales price) tax is not levied on tax as is the case with cascade taxes.

b From the government point of view the final tax, borne by goods or services, is collected in fragments as transfers are made between businesses up to final transfer to the consumer by the retailer.

c Although the tax revenue is collected in fragments, if it is wholly passed on to the consumer, through the price he pays, he eventually carries the whole burden of the tax (ie 10 per cent of the final selling price)*.

d The tax liability of each business can be seen as either 10 per cent of the difference between purchases (less tax) and sales (ie columns 1 and 3), or the difference between 10 per cent of the sale price and 10 per cent of purchase price (ie columns 4 and 5).

2.10 Taxable persons, who may include private individuals engaging in trade, are any independent sellers of taxable goods or services. Nationalised industries, and any government producing and selling agencies are included unless specifically exempted. Value added would not be identified at the

* *Thus, at the end of the day, VAT is a single tax, collected in stages, upon the value of final home consumption of goods and services. This is neither 'gross domestic product' (the total value of work done in the economy) nor is is net domestic product or net value added, ie gross domestic product less the value of capital used up during the period. It is net value added, less net additions to capital stock (for the VAT paid by the supplier is credited to the purchaser with no corresponding VAT liability), less exports, less government expenditure on wages and salaries, plus imports. This is, in fact, final domestic consumer expenditure.*

various stages of production within an integrated concern, but would be accumulated so that the concern as a whole was subject to tax on its sales to businesses outside*. Liability to VAT is independent of whether or not profits are earned in the sales transactions.

2.11 The sale of second-hand goods would not, in principle, be a taxable transaction (unless the value added by the transactor could be identified), since the value added in those goods would have been taxed when they were new, and an essential feature of the VAT is that value added should be taxed once and once only. In practice, however, the sale of second hand goods is subject to VAT in some of the countries which have adopted it.

2.12 A VAT may in principle be imposed in one of two ways. The first of these, although not adopted by any of the eight countries, is on the basis of accounts, and is known as the 'accounts' method, or sometimes the 'sales less purchases' method. Here the tax is levied on the difference between a firm's total sales in the period and the value of its purchases in the same period. Thus if VAT were imposed at a rate of 1/11 (corresponding to a rate of 10 per cent on tax-exclusive values), the value of purchases would be deducted from sales and 1/11 of the difference taken to arrive at the value added tax for that concern. If value added tax were levied at a single rate, this method would obviate the need to invoice the tax on every sale separately, and enable VAT to be calculated on the basis of the aggregate figure for sales and for purchases in each tax period.

2.13 The second method, the 'invoice' or 'tax from tax' method, which is used by all the European countries, requires each tax payer to invoice VAT separately on every sale. The tax due from a particular concern is then the VAT arising from its total sales, less a credit for the tax invoiced to it on its purchases. This is the method of imposition laid down in the EEC directives.

2.14 In Table 2 the two methods of tax imposition are illustrated for the case of a single rate of VAT charged at 10 per cent, using the invoice method, and the equivalent rate of 1/11 using the accounts method.

2.15 It is evident that there are two ways of describing the base of the VAT levied on a particular firm. It may be described as the difference between that firm's total sales excluding its exports, and its total purchases (including its purchases of capital goods but excluding its purchases of imports). On the other hand it may be described as the sum of factor incomes arising within the firm, *minus* depreciation, *minus* net capital formation and *minus* the value of exports, but *plus* the value of imports purchased by that firm. It may be that if a firm is exporting heavily, is investing a large amount in fixed capital equipment or is adding to stocks during a period, then its taxable value

* *But see paragraph 2.26.*

Table 2

		Accounts method	Invoice method	
		Final value	Tax-exclusive value	VAT invoiced
Sale by firm A direct to final consumers*		110	100	10
Sale by A to firm B*		220	200	20
Sale by B to final consumers		440	400	40
Sale by B of exports		100	100	0
A's VAT bill	$\frac{1}{11}$ of $330 = 30$		$10 + 20 = 30$	
B's VAT bill	$\frac{1}{11}$ of $(440 - 220) = 20$		$40 - 20 = 20$	
Total VAT levied	$\frac{1}{11}$ of $(770 - 220) = 50$		$30 + 20 = 50$	

* For simplicity, A is assumed to make no outside purchase (other than of imports); and B's purchases are all from A.

added for that period is negative. Using the invoice method, this is the case when the tax due on the firm's sales is less than the credit it obtains for tax invoiced to it on its total purchases.

2.16 In principle, in these cases, the firm should be able to obtain a cash refund. In practice, a so called 'buffer rule' may be applied, whereby the tax credit is carried forward and set against VAT due in the following period or periods*. In all countries an actual cash refund is granted where the credit arises because of exports. A similar situation may arise where more than one rate of VAT is in operation in which the rate of VAT applying to the sales of a particular firm is so much lower than the rate applying to its purchases that negative value added for tax purposes (ie a net credit) arises. The EEC directives state that, so far as possible, reduced rates of VAT should not be so low that this particular problem arises.

Extension of VAT to the retail stage

2.17 Although it is possible to stop applying VAT at the wholesale stage (ie with retailers, like consumers, being non-taxable persons), logically it extends right through to the final consumer. In this way all goods and services finally consumed, including the value added in retailing, are subjected to tax. Using the invoice method, the collection of the tax by instalments at each stage in the passage of goods and services to the final consumer is more fully illustrated in Table 3, again using the assumption of a single rate of 10 per cent.

The 'neutrality' of VAT

2.18 A VAT is often described as a 'neutral' tax, but this can mean a number of different things. For example, whether or not a single rate of VAT applies,

* For the operation of this in France, see Chapter 4, paragraph 4.30.

Table 3

	Purchase price to seller excluding VAT	Purchase price including VAT	VAT invoiced on purchases	Sales excluding VAT	Sales including VAT	VAT due**
A Primary producer sells to manufacturer (C)	†	—	—	100	110	10
B Plant and equipment producer sell to manufacturer (C)	†	—	—	50	55	5
C Manufacturer imports	80	88	8	—	—	1
Manufacturer exports				60	—	(24–23)
Manufacturer sells to wholesaler (D)	150‡	165	15	160	176	
D Wholesaler sells to retailer (E)	160	176	16	200	220	4 (20–16)
E Retailer sells to final consumer	200	220	20	250	275	5 (25–20)
						25

(*Note:* C's VAT bill is made up of 16 on sales to D plus 8 on imports less credit of 23 for tax paid on purchases: 15 on purchases from A and B, and 8 on imports.)

** 10 per cent on sales excluding VAT, less credit for tax invoiced on purchases.

† For simplicity it is assumed that the whole of the sales of both A and B is their own value added.

‡ From A (100) and from B (50).

It can be seen that total VAT = 25, which is 10 per cent of the value of final home consumption. Although the invoice method is used, the tax can be seen to be based, at each stage, on the difference between home sales (net of VAT) and non-import purchases (net of VAT): ie on 100, 50, 10, 40 and 50.

the tax is neutral in the sense that it does not discriminate between more and less vertically integrated methods of production*. The more a producer buys in semi-finished goods and components from a specialist outside supplier, the more he makes a pre-payment of tax invoiced to him by the supplier, and correspondingly the less tax he is accountable for himself on his own taxable value added. A small element of discrimination in favour of the vertically integrated concern survives since, by comparison with a specialist firm, its payment of VAT relating to the earlier stages of production will be delayed.

2.19 The tax is also neutral in its impact upon the turnover of two competing firms with differing ratios of labour costs to profits in their value added. Hence, its impact will be different from that of a direct tax on profits alone. This illustrates a general point that while a particular tax, considered in

* *This was a particular criticism of the cumulative cascade types of turnover tax which encouraged vertical integration in order to eliminate taxable stages in the production process.*

isolation, may be described as neutral, it is rarely the case that a switch from one tax to another is neutral, in the sense of not changing the distribution of the total final burden of taxation between two competing firms.

2.20 Neutrality in another sense, ie between different final consumer goods and services, would require that a VAT be levied at a *single* rate without any exemptions or remissions. Of particular concern is neutrality between goods on the one hand and services on the other, and between goods that are easy to tax and those that are not so easy to tax under single-stage systems. In practice, neutrality in this sense is rarely achieved (Denmark's VAT comes closest to being an exception) because more than one positive rate of VAT is normally applied (there are as many as four in France); and because, in addition, specified categories of goods and services may be exempted from VAT altogether, or other special, selective taxes may be retained.

The problems of multiple rates

2.21 The adoption of more than one rate of VAT introduces administrative complications that are not present when a single rate applies:

a No simple calculation or checking of the amount of VAT payable simply by adding up all sales and deducting all purchases is possible; individual purchases and sales have to be allocated to their appropriate tax category, and this will involve more definition and itemisation on invoices and more separate invoicing for businesses operating in more than one tax category*.

b The problem of overpayment of tax may arise for businesses whose sales are in a lower tax category than their purchases, necessitating the payment of refunds or the crediting of overpayment against future tax liabilities.

c If the invoice method is used, then it is not possible, in any straightforward way, to vary the overall burden of tax on a product by varying the rate of tax applied at various stages (eg different rates for raw and for manufactured foodstuffs or for raw wool and woollen textiles). This is because it is necessarily the rate of tax applying at the *last* stage, that sets the ratio of total VAT to total value added at all stages.

2.22 This would not be so, if it were possible to employ the sales less purchases method. In that case, the proportions of value added *at the different tax stages,* and not the rate of VAT at the final stage alone, would determine the total amount of VAT imposed on that item. However this may be in principle, it is clear that the application of more than one rate of VAT would raise serious practical problems for the sales less purchases method wherever a business is selling goods in two or more different tax categories†. In this event, purchases would require to be deducted from the sales *in the same tax category,* since it would not be practicable to deduct them from the sales to which they strictly relate as inputs. It is also obvious that a sales

* See the French VAT form in the Annex to Chapter 4.
† See Chapter 5, paragraphs 5.15–5.17.

less purchases method which allowed the effective VAT rate levied at one stage of production to be lower without simply becoming correspondingly higher at some later stage, would lead a VAT system away from neutrality between more and less vertically integrated firms.

2.23 Table 4(a) illustrates the application of dual rates of VAT (5 per cent and 10 per cent), using the invoicing method. Table 4(b) illustrates that, with the invoice method, the effective rate of tax is the last rate applying, regardless of enhanced or reduced rates at earlier stages. It also shows that this would not be the case were the accounts method employed. Table 4(c) shows that setting purchases against sales in the *same tax category* (except where the categories do not overlap, see 4(b)), is what would have to be done if the accounts method were employed in a multiple rates situation. (*Note:* In the table the rates of tax applied using the *accounts* method, are based on the difference between sales and purchases at *final* prices, ie after recovering VAT. Thus the rates equivalent to 10 per cent and 5 per cent on tax-exclusive prices are $1/11$ and $1/21$. That is to say $100 + 10$ per cent of $100 = 110$; or alternatively, 110 less $1/11$ of $110 = 110$.

2.24 From the table it can be seen that, in (b) where different rates of tax apply at different stages of the output and sale of a particular good, the element of high taxation of value added at an early stage is not removed at the last stage when using the accounts method, as it is when using the invoice method. In (c), where both sales and purchases are made at both rates of tax, if purchases are related to sales in the same tax category, using the accounts method, the two methods give identical results. There would not seem to be any need to allocate inputs to outputs for the purposes of calculating VAT by the accounts method in this dual rates case.

The treatment of exempt goods

2.25 Certain classes of transaction may be exempted from the VAT. This occurs in some countries, for example with banking and insurance services, where they are subject to separate taxes, and with certain professional services, such as those of doctors and dentists, which do not enter in an important way into the cost of taxable goods or services. The providers of exempt goods or services who are not payers of VAT are not normally entitled to recover the VAT invoiced to them on their purchases. They are not thereby penalised, since, provided the value of their sales exceeds that of their purchases, their turnover will have attracted less tax by exemption than it would have done by inclusion. (It might well be, however, that they would do even better, achieving a *net tax credit*, if they were not exempt, but paying a reduced rate. In Europe certain categories of people who originally sought exemption from VAT have for this reason subsequently asked to be included in its scope). Exemption creates a problem of double taxation, and discrimination against the exempt producer, in cases where the exempt stage is sandwiched between two taxed stages. The intervention of an untaxed stage means that the VAT levied at a prior stage is never rebated

Table 4 Effect of dual rates on the incidence of VAT

a Dual rates using the invoicing method

	Purchases excluding VAT	Purchases including VAT	VAT element in purchases	Sales excluding VAT	Sales including VAT	Net VAT due
A sells to B (10% VAT)	—	—	—	100	110	10
A sells to retailer (10% VAT)	—	—	—	50	55	5
B sells to retailer (5% VAT)	100	110	10	200	210	0
Retailer sells to consumers:						
A-type goods (10%)	50	55	5	70	77	2
B-type goods (5%)	200	210	10	280	294	4
(VAT = 10% of 70 + 5% of 280 = 21)						$\overline{21}$

b With the invoicing method the effective rate is the final rate

	Purchases excluding VAT	Purchases including VAT	Sales excluding VAT	Sales including VAT	Sales less purchases	Net VAT due
Accounts method						
A sells to B (1/11 rate)	—	—	100	110	110	10
B sells to consumers (1/21 rate)	—	110	—	215	105	5
(VAT = 10% of 100 + 5% of 100 = 15)						$\overline{15}$
Invoice method						
A sells to B (10% rate)	—	—	100	110	—	10
B sells to consumers (5% rate)	100	110	200	210	—	10 − 10 = 10
(VAT = 5% of 200 = 10)						$\overline{10}$

c With the accounts method purchases have to be set against sales in the same tax category

	Purchases excluding VAT	Purchases including VAT	Sales excluding VAT	Sales including VAT	Sales less purchases	Net VAT due
Accounts method						
A sells to C (1/11 rate)	—	—	50	55	55	5
B sells to C (1/21 rate)	—	—	100	105	105	5
C sells to consumers of goods at 1/11 rate	—	55	—	154	99	9 ⎫
C sells to consumers of goods at 1/21 rate	—	105	—	126	21	1 ⎭ 10
(VAT = 10% of 50% + 5% of 100 + 10% of 90 + 5% of 20 = 20)						$\overline{20}$
Invoice method						
A sells to C (10% rate)	—	—	50	55	—	5
B sells to C (5% rate)	—	—	100	105	—	5
C sells to consumers of goods at 10% rate ⎫	150	160	140	154	—	
C sells to consumers of goods at 5% rate ⎭			120	126		14 + 6 − 10 = 10
(VAT = 10% of 140 + 5% of 120 = 20)						$\overline{20}$

against tax due on sales at later stages. Thus, this element of value added is taxed twice, because of the intervention of the exempt stage in the whole process. This is illustrated in Table 5, assuming a 10 per cent VAT rate. In (a) B is exempt from VAT; in (b) he is not exempt.

Table 5

		Purchases excluding VAT	Purchases including VAT	Sales excluding VAT	Sales including VAT	Net VAT due
a	A sells to B	—	—	100	110	10
	B sells to C	100	110	210	—	—
	C's final sales	210	—	300	330	30
	Total VAT imposed on 300 of final sales					—
						40
b	A sells to B	—	—	100	110	10
	B sells to C	100	110	200	220	10
	C's final sales	200	220	300	330	10
						—
	Total VAT imposed on final sales of 300					30

'Captive use' production

2.26 Goods manufactured by a firm for its own use ('captive use' goods) may sometimes be subjected to tax. This needs to be done, to avoid discrimination in favour of vertical integration in cases where the *sales* of a firm are tax exempt, so that it is unable to enjoy a rebate of tax passed on to it in its outside purchases of plant and equipment, for example.

Zero rate provisions

2.27 As well as reduced rate and exempt activities, it is possible that a *zero* rate may apply to certain classes of transaction. This is a mechanism for ensuring that these transactions attract no VAT, and yet that the VAT previously paid on inputs may ultimately be recovered. In fact the zero rate applies effectively to all export transactions. The EEC directives also allow it to apply temporarily, in cases where there are special social arguments for total exemption, such as agriculture for example. A technique that may be adopted in this case is to allow the VAT-paying *purchasers* of agricultural outputs to claim a tax rebate for the notional element of tax passed on to them, through the tax-free agricultural sector, from other sectors providing agricultural inputs like fertilisers or farm machinery*.

Administration and collection of VAT

2.28 The invoicing of all sales up to the final stage of sales to final consumers, is essential to the full working of the invoicing system of the tax. Each business would normally need to be able to show the tax authorities, if required, the evidence for its claims for credit for the VAT paid by it on its purchases, and for its statement of the VAT due on its sales. The need to provide invoice proof of purchases provides an element of self enforcement in the VAT.

* *For further details, see* 'European Taxation', *Feb.* 1968.

One man's proof of purchases is evidence of another man's sales. It would be of no advantage to two taxpayers to fail to invoice a transaction between them, since this would simply make the purchaser's ultimate VAT liability correspondingly greater*. For the self enforcement to be effective it would still be necessary to make sample checks to ensure that tax credits claimed were in fact backed by purchase invoices and that the statement of sales in fact tallied with sales invoices issued. Other possibilities of tax evasion remain, for example:

a The failure to invoice sales to final consumers, or to tax-exempt purchasers, generally.

b The misclassification of goods on tax returns, where multiple rates of tax apply.

We do not suggest, however, that these would exhaust the ingenuity of tax evaders.

2.29 The attachment of a percentage for VAT to every sales invoice, and the checking of those percentages both by purchaser and by the tax authority represent a large potential administrative burden, particularly if accounting is manual, and if rates of tax are not rounded. Conversely, the burden would be significantly reduced, though not abolished, with machine accounting, and with rates of VAT like 5, 10 or 20 per cent. The problem remains of how to deal with small businesses, such as small retail outlets, where books are not kept in sufficient detail for the tax due on sales or reclaimable on purchases to be proved. One device for dealing with the problem is to estimate their turnover, and to allow businesses with very low turnover to have the option of keeping the necessary books of account and being inducted into the VAT system, or of staying outside it, receiving no credits, and being subject to a 'forfeit' tax, related to estimated turnover.

2.30 A 'taxable event' or transaction is normally pinpointed at the moment when goods are delivered or services rendered, and the tax falls due for payment at the end of the tax period within which the event occurs. In practice, tax collection may be related to either invoice dates or settlement dates. Tax returns may be required each month, or at longer intervals such as each quarter or half year, for reasons of convenience. Collected at relatively short intervals, a VAT contrasts with a single late-stage tax like purchase tax in the following respect: the tax receipt accrues during the process of production as contributions to the final good are provided for sale by intermediate producers. It may be noted that methods of collection may be employed which do not require the computation of the exact amount of tax due on the collection date: eg, in France, an option exists whereby the tax charged each month is one twelfth of the previous full year's tax, with an adjustment up or down at the end of the year.

---

* *This point while not accepted by the revenue departments in this country was nevertheless stressed by officials in the French and German Ministries of Finance.*

2.31 The *collection* of a VAT is in principle distinct from its verification and control- ie from *inspection*. As collection needs to be at fairly frequent intervals, it is, in the European countries which have adopted the tax, universally based on periodic returns by the individual tax-payers. That is to say, statements are filed of tax due on sales, of the credits claimed for tax invoiced on purchases and of the net VAT payment owing; and payment must be made shortly thereafter. Verification of the tax paid may be done annually and need not be carried out by the department responsible for the collection of the tax. This verification typically requires inspection of at least some of the same accounts that are needed for the assessment of business income tax and corporation tax, albeit in a more detailed form if multiple rates of VAT or exemptions apply.

The incidence of VAT

2.32 The final incidence of the VAT is not part of its general characteristics. Although the tax is automatically invoiced on sales, the impact of its imposition upon the tax-exclusive prices of goods and services will depend upon the state of competition in particular markets, upon the powers of particular taxpayers to vary prices, and upon what associated changes are introduced in other taxes at the same time*.

* *When VAT was introduced in West Germany in 1968, we were told there that, for example, the effect on the price index was much less than would have been the case had the tax simply been shifted forward with no adjustment of tax-exclusive prices. This has been explained by the pressure of competition at a time of generally depressed business activity, but must also have been due to the removal of other taxes.*

Characteristics of UK taxation 3

Note: *Most of the figures in this report have been based on the most recent tax data available, in most cases 1969. However, some of the calculations in Chapter 5 of incidence effects of substitution of VAT for existing taxes were based on 1967 data and it has not been possible to revise these. The most significant changes to be kept in mind since 1967 are the increases in corporation tax, purchase tax and SET whose yield has now increased very substantially, and which would, therefore, require more revenue from any alternative tax if they were to be replaced.*

At the same time, however, the gross tax base to which a VAT would be applied has also increased from the £25,000 million of 1967 to possibly £31,000–£32,000 million in 1970/71.

	1967 £ million	1970/71 Estimates £ million
Corporation tax	1,147	1,900*
Purchase tax	748	1,260
SET (net)†	434	917

* A cut in the rate of corporation tax from 45 per cent to 42½ per cent will reduce the figure by perhaps £60 million.

† This figure includes the net yield from the private sector and public corporations, together with payments made by central government and local authorities.

3.1 The case for considering the adoption of a value added tax in the UK depends not only on the merits and likely effects of a VAT itself, but also on the view taken of the efficiency, equity and economic effects of existing taxation arrangements. This view must have regard not only to current considerations but also to anticipated future developments in the growth of the economy and the Government's social objectives and revenue requirements. If the present arrangements are thought to meet satisfactorily the present and anticipated demands placed on them, then the case for changing them is weakened.

The changing structure of UK taxation

3.2 There are certain immediate difficulties which arise in considering the present structure of UK fiscal arrangements, because in recent years there have been considerable changes in the structure and level of taxation which have been determined essentially by the needs of short term economic management. The financial needs of the government would in any case have required increased taxation, because in the economic situation of the past few years a budget deficit above the line was not desirable. However, in selecting the type of taxation which was imposed, short term economic management and longer term economic and political aims were, as far as possible, combined. Corporation tax (introduced in 1966) and the selective employment tax (introduced from 5 September 1966) were cases in point. SET, for instance, has a built-in selectivity which was aimed at redistributing manpower and, to some extent, at supporting regional development policy, while corporation tax involves the differential treatment of retained and distributed profits.

3.3 As may be seen from Table 6 total central government taxation in 1969 amounted to 27·5 per cent of GNP at market prices, and central government revenue was 32·4 per cent. Of the former slightly more revenue was raised by taxes on income than by taxes on expenditure. The change in the structure of taxation in the UK since 1955 is shown in Table 7.

3.4 The 1969 distribution of total tax revenue between income and expenditure moved a little towards expenditure. However the 1970/71 estimates suggest that this movement has now been reversed.

Table 6   Structures of UK taxation, 1969

	£ million		Percentage of total central government revenue	
Taxes on income				
Income tax	4,779		32·4	
Surtax	240		1·6	
Corporation tax*	1,317		8·9	
Total	6,336	6,336	42·9	42·9
Taxes on expenditure				
Tobacco	1,165		7·9	
Alcohol	855		5·8	
Hydrocarbon oils	1,278		8·6	
Purchase tax	1,110		7·5	
Import duties	221		1·5	
Motor vehicle licences	431		2·9	
SET	808		5·5	
Other†	326		2·2	
Total	6,194	6,194	41·9	41·9
Total tax revenue		12,530		84·8
National Insurance contributions etc		2,243	15·2	15·2
of which: Employers NI only		1,051		
Employees NI only		939		
Total central government revenue		14,773		100
Local authority rates		1,674		
Total revenue and rates		16,447		
GNP at market prices		45,625		
As percentage of GNP at market prices:				
Total revenue and rates			36·0	
Total central government revenue			32·4	
Total central government taxes			27·5	
Local authority rates			3·7	
NI contributions			4·9	

* Corporation tax and profits tax, less overspill relief.

† Temporary charge on imports, betting, stamp duties, post office contributions to exchequer, and miscellaneous, less export rebates.

Table 7　Change in structure of UK central government taxation since 1955

	1955	1960	1965	1969	1970/71 (est)
Taxes on income (%)*	51·6	51·0	51·7	50·6	52·9
Taxes on expenditure (%)	48·4	49·0	48·3	49·4	47·1
Total taxes	100·0	100·0	100·0	100·0	100·0
Taxes as percentage of GNP†	23·3	20·8	21·8	27·5	28·0
Taxes and social security contributions as percentage of GNP†	26·4	24·3	26·5	32·4	33·4
of which					
a Employers SSC	1·5	1·7	2·2	2·2	—
b Employees SSC	1·5	1·7	2·2	2·2	—
c Self-employed etc SSC	0·2	0·2	0·2	0·2	—
SSC (%)	11·7	14·6	17·8	15·2	16·0
Total taxes (%)	88·3	85·4	82·2	84·8	84·0
Total taxes and SSC	100·0	100·0	100·0	100·0	100·0

Sources: 1955/69: National Income and Expenditure 'Blue Book', 1966 and 1970. 1970/71 estimates from Financial Statement.

* Including corporation tax and profits tax less overspill relief.

† GNP at market prices, expenditure method; NEDO estimates for 1970/71.

Some international tax comparisons

3.5　Figures of this kind cannot prove or disprove any judgements about the efficiency or equity of the tax system. Neither is the readily available comparative international data a very useful measure for this purpose. The total amount of taxation which is levied, and the way in which it is distributed, is a function of the institutional arrangements which exist in the country; the size and nature of the public sector, the financial relations between central and local governments, the preferred methods of financing, and so on. Different countries adopt different conventions in accounting, their income structures and expenditure patterns are different, and their social and political preferences as between individual and collective consumption vary from time to time and from place to place. Nevertheless, a conventional comparison is given in Table 8 so as to set the broad structure of central and local government taxation in the UK beside that in other countries at a comparable stage of economic development.

3.6　A cautious summing up of these figures, and various other international comparisons which have been made*, suggests that the overall burden of taxation on the UK economy is not exceptionally high as compared with other countries. Indeed, in relation to consideration of a VAT, one of the most surprising features in the table is the fact that this country is near to the top of the league in the proportion of revenue raised by taxes on expenditure. This arises primarily because of the inclusion of local

* *A recent attempt to make international tax comparisons less ambiguous is a* PEP *study by C V Brown and D A Dawson* 'Personal Taxation, Incentives and Reform', Jan., *1969.*

Table 8 International comparison of taxation in 14 OECD countries 1968

| | Total taxes (including social security) | | Total taxes (excluding social security) | | Taxes on incomes | | | | | | | |
| | | | | | Household | | | | Corporations | | | |
	% of GNP	Rank	% of GNP	Rank	% of total taxes*	Rank	% of GNP	Rank	% of total taxes*	Rank	% of GNP	Rank
Austria	43·2	2	33·5	4	27·8	8	12·0	5	4·9	11	2·1	9
Belgium	37·4	9	26·6	10	24·6	10	9·2	10	6·3	8	2·3	8
Canada	36·4	10	32·4	5	28·2	7	10·3	8	12·5	3	4·5	2
Denmark	40·8	6	38·6	2	44·2	1	18·0	2	2·9	14	1·2	14
France	42·5	4	25·8	11	12·8	14	5·4	13	5·0	10	2·1	9
Germany	39·8	8	27·7	7	23·8	11	9·5	9	6·5	7	2·6	6
Italy	34·1	11	21·7	12	16·6	13	5·7	12	5·7	9	1·9	11
Japan	20·3	14	16·5	14	20·6	12	4·2	14	21·1	1	4·3	3
Netherlands	42·2	5	27·2	8	27·5	9	11·6	7	7·3	5	3·1	4
Norway	42·7	3	32·4	5	32·2	5	13·7	3	3·9	12	1·7	13
Sweden	48·4	1	39·0	1	44·1	2	21·3	1	3·7	13	1·8	12
Switzerland	24·2	13	18·9	13	36·3	3	8·8	11	10·3	4	2·5	7
United States	32·9	12	27·0	9	36·2	4	11·9	6	15·6	2	5·1	1
UK	40·1	7	34·2	3	30·9	6	12·4	4	7·2	6	2·9	5

Source: Economic Trends, August 1970 (based on OECD National Accounts).

GNP is here taken at factor cost (cf Table 6, at market prices).

* Including social security contributions.

government rates (i e a tax on the possession and use of housing) in this category in order to achieve international comparability in the field of local taxation. If rates are excluded from the UK figures the proportion of total taxes raised on expenditure drops from 47·2 per cent to about 38 per cent. It will also be noted the UK is nearest to the bottom of the table in respect of the importance of social security contributions; the counterpart of this is, of course, that general taxation will be relatively more important.

3.7 Aggregated figures naturally cannot throw light on the final incidence of taxation as between different groups and sectors in the economy. It does seem, however, from various studies which have been made that the total burden of taxation in the UK falls relatively heavily on the lower and the higher income groups, while a very wide band of middle incomes are taxed at about the same level as in other countries and at a rate broadly proportional to income. To put it another way the tax system itself is regressive at the lower levels, proportional in the middle, and progressive at the upper end. However, the effect of Government transfer payments, in cash and kind, is to reduce the burden of taxation for the lower income groups.

Direct taxation in relation to VAT

3.8 The question of the relationship of a VAT to the direct personal taxation of individuals has not occupied a central place in this study. Nevertheless,

Taxes on expenditure				Social security contributions								
				Total				Paid by employers				
% of total taxes*	Rank	% of GNP	Rank	% of total taxes*	Rank	% of GNP	Rank	% of total taxes*	Rank	% of GNP	Rank	
44·9	4	19·4	1	22·4	7	9·7	7	18·8	3	8·1	3	Austria
40·3	7	15·1	9	28·8	5	10·8	5	18·3	4	6·8	4	Belgium
48·4	1	17·6	5	10·9	13	4·0	12	6·0	12	2·2	11	Canada
47·4	2	19·4	1	5·5	14	2·2	14	2·1†	13	0·8†	13	Denmark
42·9	5	18·3	4	39·3	1	16·7	1	28·1	1	11·9	1	France
39·3	10	15·7	8	30·4	4	12·1	4	15·6	5	6·2	5	Germany
41·3	6	14·1	10	36·4	2	12·4	3	—	—	—	—	Italy
39·6	9	8·0	13	18·7	10	3·8	13	11·5	7	2·3	10	Japan
29·6	14	12·5	11	35·5	3	15·0	2	26·1	2	11·0	2	Netherlands
39·8	8	17·0	6	24·1	6	10·3	6	12·3	6	5·3	6	Norway
32·9	11	15·9	7	19·4	9	9·4	8	10·1	8	4·9	7	Sweden
31·4	12	7·6	14	22·0	8	5·3	11	7·6	10	1·8	12	Switzerland
30·4	13	10·0	12	17·8	11	5·8	10	9·2	9	3·0	8	United States
47·2	3	18·9	3	14·7	12	5·9	9	7·5	11	3·0	8	UK

† No figure for social security contributions by employers is available for Denmark in 1968. An estimate has been made assuming the proportion of total social security contributions to be the same as for 1967. The estimated figure is 667 million kroner.

it is such a major element in our fiscal arrangements, and it looms so large in any discussion of taxation questions, that in considering a major change in the tax structure, such as a VAT would involve, the possibility of consequential changes in income tax cannot realistically be excluded. Personal income tax and surtax not only provided about 34 per cent of total central government tax revenue in 1969, but they are the principal progressive element in our tax system making for the reduction of inequalities of income.

3.9 Several aspects of personal taxation might be considered in a situation in which a VAT was introduced. First, there are two general, subjective and theoretical considerations:

a A view that high marginal rates of income tax may have disincentive effects, not only on those earning the incomes taxed at high marginal rates, but also by reducing the willingness of persons to take risks in order to reach these income brackets.

b That after a certain level of minimum incomes has been reached and after a desired degree of redistribution has been effected by direct taxation, there may be a case for switching the emphasis of taxation, away from earnings and on to expenditure.

3.10 Three more specific points are:

a As money incomes rise, and regardless of what is happening to real incomes, more and more people enter the categories of taxable income for the first time or move into higher tax brackets. Some adjustment of levels of allowances is likely to become necessary in any case if a steadily rising proportion of incomes is not to be taken in direct taxes.

b As a consequence of a VAT there would inevitably be changes in relative prices for which some compensatory measures would need to be taken and part of these might be appropriately dealt with by changes in personal direct taxes and benefits.

c If adjustments were being made to corporate taxation as part of the VAT package, some consideration might have to be given to personal taxation, to provide equivalent adjustments in the unincorporated business sector.

The type and size of the changes that might be desirable would depend on whether the present distribution of post-tax (direct and indirect) income is to be maintained or whether it is to be altered.

3.11 Corporation tax is currently levied at a rate similar to, or marginally lower than, in other countries. It yields about 9 per cent of current tax revenue. There has been, for many years, considerable debate as to whether direct taxes of this kind enter into the pricing policy calculations of companies: if they do not then, for example, no encouragement to exports due to price reductions would arise from a reduction in such taxes. This latter view influenced the Richardson Committee in reaching its conclusions that a change from profits tax to VAT would not be advantageous. It is still widely held, but there is some justification for taking a different view: empirical academic research is inconclusive, one way or the other, but more important, the introduction of more sophisticated methods of accounting in industry— which are spreading rapidly—has resulted in closer attention than before being paid to post-tax measurements of profitability*. Moreover, the role of the profitable price leader, who would benefit most from a cut in corporation tax, should not be underestimated as a factor in determining an industry's pricing structure.

3.12 With the exception of this above mentioned corporation tax issue, this study does not concern itself in detail with direct taxation.

Indirect taxation on consumers' expenditure

3.13 Table 9 opposite shows the incidence of indirect taxation on consumer expenditure in 1969, on the assumption that indirect taxation on industry is passed forward in prices.

3.14 This table, incomplete as it is, demonstrates the narrow base of indirect taxation, net of subsidies, in the UK. The first group, accounting for 20 per cent of consumer expenditure in 1969, produced 70 per cent of the allocated

* *It is possible that exports might benefit without reductions in prices from an increase in the post tax rate of return on assets employed in exporting, thus justifying increased selling effort and risk taking in export markets.*

indirect tax revenue, while at the other extreme the group accounting for 53 per cent of consumer expenditure, produced only 7 per cent of the revenue. (As the footnote to Table 9 points out, however, about one third of total indirect tax revenue has not been allocated to specific expenditures, and this if it could be accurately allocated would reduce the extreme disparities to some extent.)

3.15 Although the average incidence of taxation on expenditure in the second group was 13–14 per cent, there was a considerable variation in the burden from nil for some goods to about 37 per cent for consumer durables, cars, electrical goods, etc, and 55 per cent in the case of furs, perfumes, etc.

3.16 The (very low) tax yield in the large third category, which includes expenditure on food, is almost wholly accounted for by purchase tax on a very few items and by SET—which taxes part of the service element.

Table 9   Taxes on consumers' expenditure at current market prices in 1969*

	Tax £ million	%	Expenditure £ million	%	Tax as a percentage of expenditure
Tobacco	1,167		1,694		68·9
Alcohol etc	826		1,824		45·3
Motor running	745		1,518		49·1
	2,738	70·1	5,036	20·2	54·4
Durables	346		1,957		17·7
Other household goods	68		839		8·1
Chemists' goods	93		422		22·0
Clothing	215		2,417		8·9
Recreational goods	78		637		12·2
Miscellaneous goods	95		359		26·5
	895	22·9	6,631	26·5	13·5
Food	−2		5,977		†
Fuel and light	7		1,421		0·5
Travel	−7		924		−0·8
Communications	1		284		0·4
Books etc	4		420		1·0
Entertainment	28		472		5·9
Other services (including catering)	241		3,831		6·3
	272	7·0	13,329	53·3	2·0
Total of above	3,905*	100·0	24,996	100·0	15·6

* Total expenditure taxes were £6,194 million (see Table 6). The difference between this figure and the £3,905 million above is largely accounted for by the non-allocation in the table of part of oil duties not relating to consumer petrol, certain import duties, motor vehicles licences, part of SET and purchase tax not falling directly on final consumer expenditure, and also some miscellaneous taxes and duties.

† = Less than ±0·05.

3.17 The heavy taxation falling on tobacco (over two thirds of expenditure) and alcohol (just under half of expenditure) is in part a reflection of social attitudes to the consumption of these goods, but also to their extreme buoyancy as revenue raisers in the past. There is doubt whether this can be relied upon in the future, and further increases in revenue from this source are likely to be small. To a considerable extent further increases in taxation on tobacco and alcohol have recently been replaced by a variety of taxes on vehicles of all kinds, and on petrol and oil—both for private and commercial road transport.

3.18 The quite heavy dependence of the UK upon indirect taxes (which include, in the international statistics, all local rates and taxes) in comparison with other countries (referred to in Table 8 and paragraph 3.6) has been associated with a rather low proportion of non-specific ad valorem taxes on expenditure. An international comparison of the structure of indirect taxes, excluding local rates, is set out in Table 10.

Table 10   Weight of certain specific taxes in UK compared with other countries (1968)

As % of total tax	UK	Denmark	France	Germany	Nether-lands	Sweden	USA
Tobacco	7·3	6·1	1·6	3·1	2·4	2·7	0·8
Alcoholic drinks	5·3	5·2	0·9	1·7	1·4	4·4	1·6
Hydrocarbon oils	7·3	3·8	3·5	5·1	4·3	3·2	1·3
Total	19·9	15·1	6·0	9·8	8·0	10·3	3·7
Total indirect taxes	47·2	47·4	41·2	37·0	29·6	32·9	30·4
Total indirect *excluding* tobacco, drinks, oils	27·2	32·3	35·2	27·2	21·6	22·6	26·7
Total tax as percentage of GNP at *factor cost*	40·1	40·8	44·3	42·3	42·2	48·4	32·9
Taxes on tobacco, drinks, oils as percentage of total indirect taxes	42·3	31·9	14·6	26·5	27·2	31·2	12·1

Sources: HM Customs and Excise and OECD National Accounts 1950/68.

This shows the unusual extent to which the UK indirect tax system relies upon the collection of specific duties on a narrow group of goods: tobacco, alcoholic drinks and hydrocarbon oils, and the correspondingly slight reliance upon general ad valorem taxes whose yields rise in proportion to the value of expenditure as prices are rising. The first two of these categories of goods—tobacco and alcoholic drink—account to a very large extent for the regressive effect (increasing income inequality) of indirect taxes as a whole. The third—the hydrocarbon oil duties—have the disadvantage that they are levied upon purchases by producers as well as consumers. This means that although their incidence is widely and thinly spread they find their way into industrial costs including exports and investment goods.

3.19 Purchase tax, now levied at four rates, is based on the selective taxation of goods, primarily those entering into personal consumption. It is weighted heavily towards the taxation of consumer durables, such as motor cars, and electrical appliances. These are taxed at the second highest of the current four rates, which yields about half of purchase tax revenue. It is a tax whose contribution to policy as an economic regulator is increasingly being questioned, because (like the tobacco and alcohol duty) there is no clear evidence that to increase it necessarily decreases *total* consumption in real terms while it discriminates heavily against particular industries.

Indirect taxation on industry

3.20 Indirect taxes paid by industry and business* in 1969 are estimated to have been as follows:

	£ million
SET (net)	808
Hydrocarbon oil tax	685
Motor licensing	187
Purchase tax (part)	138

* Except for SET, figures show total tax paid less allocations to consumers' expenditure, public sector current spending and half allocations to domestic fixed capital formation.
Source: Economic Trends, November 1970.

If these taxes were passed forward in prices, as has been assumed in Table 9, it is estimated that they would have increased home prices by about 7–8 per cent. Also, because in contrast to a VAT they could not be rebated on exports under the rules of GATT (which require that the tax element should be capable of precise identification), they would also have increased export prices or reduced the profitability of exporting.

3.21 SET is designed to impose taxation on distribution and services, to encourage the transfer of scarce manpower into manufacturing, and to assist in regional restructuring. It can, therefore, be viewed as the beginning of the general taxation on services to bring it into line with taxation on goods, and also as widening the base of indirect taxation. However, because it taxes distribution it also imposes additional taxation on goods as well as services. Moreover, the way in which it is administered involves large flows of money from and to industry as well as temporarily reduced company liquidity; also because of its selectivity between industries and because its incidence is assessed partly by the nature of occupancy of buildings, it has created many anomalies and borderline cases which have been the subject of wide-spread criticism.

Effect of taxation and benefits on income distribution

3.22 One of the effects of a deliberately progressive taxation system is to reduce the inequalities that exist in pre-tax incomes, and this is reinforced by the payment of direct benefits to certain sections of the population through

29

pensions, family allowances etc. It is difficult to measure the income effects of these flows to and from the Government, but various estimates have been made and their broad conclusions are as follows:

a The major contribution to the reduction of income inequality is provided by social benefits.

b Direct taxation is also progressive.

c Indirect taxation is regressive overall. Some indirect taxes such as those on motoring, wines and spirits, and many durable items, are broadly progressive, but those on beer and tobacco are quite heavily regressive, and the total incidence of purchase tax is also mildly regressive. Moreover, despite their high degree of selectivity, our indirect taxes are likely to become less progressive as the enjoyment of consumer durables, once unequivocally luxuries, becomes increasingly more general.

3.23 The most relevant conclusions are that no very significant effect on income distribution in either direction results from taxation alone, but that it is necessary to consider taxation in conjunction with social benefits to see how the system as a whole affects income inequality (and, indeed, other social or economic objectives). (See also paragraphs 5.52–5.58.)

Conclusion

3.24 This sketch of the UK tax system suggests that, by international standards, the country does not at present bear an unusually high burden of taxation (including social security contributions) relative to GNP. Moreover, while indirect taxation as a whole provides a large share of revenue, ad valorem, non-specific, expenditure taxes provide quite a small share. In consequence, an expansion of the indirect tax base at a suitable rate, or rates, would not produce an unrealistic relationship to national output nor grossly distort the range and pattern of current taxation on expenditure. At the same time there may be a need when instigating a major tax change, such as a VAT, to take other taxes into account: in particular, personal taxation at the higher and at the lower ranges, purchase tax and also SET. We have seen, too, that indirect taxes falling on industry are a burden on exporters, which might be avoided by a VAT if it were accompanied by appropriate changes in other taxes. The net effect of such a package of changes would always have to be scrutinised from the point of view of income distribution, and appropriate corrective measures taken. The role of specific charges and subsidies in selectively encouraging or discouraging the production and consumption of certain commodities should also be weighed against the merit of tax neutrality between commodities.

VAT in Europe   4

4.1 The reason for the introduction of the VAT system by the countries of the European Economic Community is that it provides a method of turnover taxation which can eliminate tax frontiers. The multi-stage turnover taxes previously used by several of them created difficulties in the adjustment of taxes on goods involved in foreign trade. However, in the course of discussing and then actually implementing the VAT, it was additionally discovered by EEC members and by the Scandinavian countries who have more recently adopted the system, that it had other positive characteristics of its own. Among these was its neutrality, its ability to broaden the tax base as compared with single-stage wholesale taxes, and it was also an improvement in many ways on the cascade type of turnover tax such as existed in Germany. Moreover, by being a general tax on expenditure, it should favour savings and, to the extent that it replaced taxes which formerly fell on capital goods and exports, it seemed to offer some encouragement to investment and assistance to the balance of payments.

4.2 The adoption of a 'common system of tax on value added' by the Council of the EEC on 9 February 1967, with the general application of the tax due by 1 January 1970, was preceded by long and extensive discussions. In April 1954 France had adopted a value added tax up to the wholesale level as part of its tax reforms in 1954/55. This VAT was not complete by today's standards, as it applied essentially to the transactions of manufacturers and wholesalers, but stopped short of the retail stage and services. These two activities were, however, separately taxed. The final step was taken by France thirteen years later, on 1 January 1968, in order to comply with the First and Second Directives of the Council of the EEC.

4.3 Seven countries in Europe have practical experience of a complete VAT system covering retail trade and services as well as the manufacturing sector. These are Denmark (effective since 3 July 1967), France and Germany (both effective from 1 January 1968), the Netherlands and Sweden (effective as of 1 January 1969) and Norway and Luxembourg who adopted VAT on 1 January 1970. Belgium introduced the system on 1 January 1971 after having been granted a one year extension of the original deadline by the Third Directive of 9 December 1969. Italy, also under this Directive, is due to introduce VAT on 1 January 1972. There it is proposed to extend a limited cascade system covering wholesale transactions to replace a range of excise taxes, and to reform the income tax. Ireland also intends to introduce VAT in 1972. The lessons learnt from the real practical experience of VAT have led to modifications of both the legal and the administrative systems of the more experienced countries and has, at least to some extent, been incorporated into those of the countries which have introduced VAT. Simplification and streamlining has been the overall aim.

4.4 The initial version of the Community's First Draft Directive on the harmonisation of the tax laws of member states was submitted to the Council

31

of Ministers by the EEC Commission on 5 November 1962. It underwent several amendments and modifications before the one stage introduction of VAT was finally approved in 1967. At the same time the Second Directive (originally submitted in 1965), on the measures pertaining to the structure and methods for applying the common system VAT, was also adopted. The legal seal of the EEC Commission on both Directives marked the transition from the theoretical, ideological and political discussion to that of the problems of practical application.

4.5 That these practical applications have not yet been fully solved is shown by the variety of practices found within the EEC countries themselves, especially with regard to different rates of tax, but also in respect of more detailed measures such as coverage and exemptions. This lack of uniformity is recognised by the EEC Council, to which biennial reports on the functioning of VAT are to be submitted, the first on 1 January 1972, so that further steps can be taken towards tax harmonisation. The long term aim of the EEC concerns not only VAT but the totality of taxation and envisages the eventual harmonisation of tax rates as well as tax structures.

Rates of VAT in Europe

4.6 There is a general consensus of opinion in Europe, that a single rate VAT, if at all possible, is preferable to a multiple rate system. This is basically because it is easier to administer, but there is also the added reason that a

Table 11 Effective VAT rates

	Standard rate %	Reduced rate %	Intermediate rate %	Sumptuary rate %
Belgium[1]	18·00	6·0	14·00	25·00
Denmark[2]	15·00	—	—	—
France[3]	23·00	7·5	17·60	33·33
Germany	11·00	5·5	—	—
Luxembourg[4]	10·00	5·0	—	—
Netherlands[5]	14·00	4·0	—	—
Norway[6]	20·00	—	—	—
Sweden[7]	17·65	—	—	—

[1] Introduced 1 January 1971: the 14 per cent and the 18 per cent rates will be increased to 15 per cent and 20 per cent on 1 January 1972.

[2] The original rate was 10 per cent; from April 1968 to June 1970 12·5 per cent applied.

[3] These rates were introduced on 1 January 1970 and were set to correspond as closely as possible to the former tax-inclusive rates.

[4] Original rates 8 and 4 per cent; a 2 per cent 'exceptional' rate applicable to items especially important in the cost of living was introduced for a transition period and is still in force.

[5] The standard rate was raised from 12 per cent on 1 January 1971.

[6] The rate can be revised annually.

[7] The tax-inclusive rate is 15 per cent (previously 10 per cent) as of 1 January 1971.

[8] Likely to be raised later to 15 per cent.

single rate is the most neutral from an economic point of view. If selectivity in the system is desired, several rates or a similar device, would be required. In fact, and despite its advantages, only Denmark, Norway and Sweden have adopted a single rate. Italy also intends to adopt a single rate to begin with, reviewing it after two years. The other countries have, or are introducing, two or more rates. These are mainly the result of the need to satisfy political and/or social criteria which could not be satisfied sufficiently by other methods, such as selective exemptions from VAT (eg doctors' services), assimilation of existing indirect taxation, and/or adjustments of existing direct taxation and allowance systems.

4.7 The comparison of rates of tax in different countries has been simplified, as now only in Sweden is VAT included in the tax base. (If the VAT rate is 10 per cent, then an article selling for £100 *tax-exclusive,* attracts tax of £10 making the selling price, *tax-inclusive,* £110; but the VAT element is £10, which is 1/11th or 9·1 per cent of the *tax-inclusive* price.) In Table 11 the rates are given for the VAT base exclusive of the tax. The tax-exclusive rates are also used for the comparison because they are the rates which are applied on imports, which have not, of course, previously been subject to the VAT of the country in question.

4.8 France stopped charging VAT on tax-inclusive prices as a simplification measure from 1 January 1970. (Certain other specified taxes are, however, still in force and are collected parallel with VAT.) This and some administrative reforms were undertaken in response to complaints from retailers that VAT was too complicated.

4.9 In Sweden there is a lower rate for the import of prefabricated houses, at an effective 6·38 per cent rate (or 6 per cent VAT inclusive). On the same principle as Denmark, this is done in order to bring the import rate on a par with the domestic rate where a reduction of the VAT burden is achieved by means of a reduction of the taxable base.

4.10 Both France and Sweden use the device of a reduced taxable base on certain categories of goods. In France it applies to books, which receive a 30 per cent rebate, and to land, which enjoys a two thirds rebate. In Sweden the taxable base of buildings is reduced by 40 per cent, and for services in connection with water supplies, roads, streets, bridges, railways, harbours, canals, and other waterways, the taxable base is reduced by 80 per cent.

4.11 This device of a reduction of the taxable base rather than the use of differential rates for certain items is an interesting element in the VAT tax system. In Sweden it was introduced in order to obtain neutrality of choice when deciding whether to use direct labour (both for individuals and, more important, local authorities) or to contract out the project. The reduced taxable base might prove to have advantages of presentation or flexibility in the levying of VAT on certain items in comparison with the use of differential rates.

4.12 The only departure from the principle of neutral rates of VAT on domestic and imported goods were the German emergency measures taken in connection with the financial crisis in November 1968. For the period 29 November 1968 to 28 October 1969, a special refund was granted in respect of those imported goods subject to taxation at importation. At the same time similar taxes at similar rates were put on exports. These measures, which were seen as a substitute for the revaluation of the Deutsch-mark, were exceptional measures to meet a crisis situation and not a normal 'regulatory' aspect of VAT.

4.13 Thus, in all countries, domestic and imported goods are generally subject to similar rates of VAT. However, as will be shown below, variations in coverage, exemptions and times of payment mean that the principle of harmonisation of taxes, both inside and outside the EEC, has even farther to go than the diversity of rates suggest.

The coverage of VAT in Europe

4.14 In principle the VAT is paid on the full value to the final buyer (or direct consumer) of the costs of raw materials, production, transport, and services involved in the item being purchased. As the intermediate stages of production obtain a credit for tax paid on the value added at each earlier stage, the incidence of the tax is theoretically on the final consumer. If not only the rates but also the coverage of, and exemptions from, the tax were identical in all the countries concerned, their full tax harmonisation would be achieved, at least so far as VAT is concerned.

4.15 Each country usually has a complicated definition of the national territory in which VAT is paid. The obvious rules are, however, that it applies to all entrepreneurs irrespective of nationality, resident within the national frontiers. (Bonded warehouses—which include tax free shops at airports—are an obvious exception.)

4.16 The scope of the VAT is usually defined as:
a The delivery of goods, leasing, and the rendering of services, all within the country, against payment by entrepreneurs in the course of their business operations.
b Certain self-deliveries and the rendering of certain services for one's own benefit.
c The importation of goods including the cost of insurance and freight and customs or other duties and/or taxes, if any.

4.17 In all countries exports and usually their transport are not liable to VAT. The regulations covering the extent to which services for export purposes (eg architectural and engineering designs for constructions to be erected abroad) are freed from VAT vary; the basic principle seems to be similar to that applying to merchandise exports. In some countries special arrangements apply to re-exports and/or the imports of goods for re-export.

4.18 The main broad sector exempted from VAT in all countries is banking and financial services, in which there are institutions where a value added cannot readily be ascribed to the transactions. In some countries these organisations, which may include insurance companies, are subject to special taxes. The same considerations sometimes apply to land, buildings and rents where national practices also vary widely.

4.19 In several countries the liberal professions are partially (through reduced rates), or wholly, exempted from VAT. In Germany and Denmark, for example, provisions are made for certain professional persons to choose for themselves whether to join the VAT system. The inducement is that they can themselves obtain credit for their own purchases of goods and services. According to the preamble of the EEC Council's Second Directive, it is left to the Member States themselves to determine the rules concerning the various services whose cost does not influence the price of goods. (Some guidance is, however, given in the Second Directive in Article 6, Items 1–4, and Annex B.)

However, an *employed* person, even when exercising a liberal profession, eg accountant, architect, engineer (ie not self-employed), is nowhere subject to VAT.

4.20 All countries have, for social, political and/or economic reasons, made exceptions for some or most of the following items, either totally or at the final consumer stage when there is then no refund for accumulated tax credits. This list, however, is not exhaustive, and it includes only some of the most usual exemptions as an indication of the range of items for which special provision may have to be made.
Sea-going vessels (sometimes including fishing boats)
Certain aircraft (usually internationally operated) and aircraft parts
The services on these ships and aircraft
Medicines for sale by prescription and/or for use in hospitals
Preserved human blood and mother's milk
Broadcasting and television
Newspapers and/or publications of various kinds
Works of art when sold and/or imported by the artist
Travellers' samples
Medical services (and sometimes undertaker services)
Services rendered by non-profit making sporting organisations
Certain educational services (ie lectures and similar services provided the fees serve mainly to cover expenses)
Services by certain charities.

The three countries which have had a full VAT in force for some time have either made, or are contemplating, adjustments to their exemptions lists according to experience; VAT, like any tax system, can be modified.

4.21 France has some exemptions not present in other countries. These include certain transactions connected with the sale of livestock and fish, and of co-operative societies; the sale of second hand goods (even industrial products such as new rejects and recovered materials); but since 1 December 1968, second hand car sales have been subject to VAT. (In Sweden they are exempted.) Entertainments, shows and games are exempted from VAT in France, but have their own special taxation. Transactions of certain official bodies, not financially independent, are also not liable to VAT, while the sale of goods subject to State monopoly (eg tobacco and matches) are not liable at the retail stage.

4.22 The manner in which the countries applying multiple rates have distinguished between items qualifying for reduced rates are so individual that the details cannot be given in a brief survey, but the general pattern is to distinguish necessities, eg food, attracting a low or nil-rate; standard items including utilities, at an intermediate rate; and luxuries, usually taxed at the highest rate. The classification reflects historical and social factors, as often as economic criteria.

4.23 All the countries have tried to keep the number of exemptions down to the minimum, and Denmark, Sweden and Norway have the shortest lists. This is partly the result of the experience obtained in France, where a limited VAT up to the wholesale stage has been operating since 1954/55; it was imposed there on top of the complicated existing indirect taxation structure and considerable efforts have since been made to get rid of certain low revenue and high administrative cost taxes, the main reforms having been made just before or in connection with the extension of VAT to the retail and service stage. The administrative burden of long lists of exemptions (as well as multiple rates), is such that the Scandinavian countries have all opted for the simplest possible systems, compatible with their other national objectives.

Administrative arrangements

4.24 None of the European countries which have introduced VAT appear to have experienced any insuperable administrative problems. Some temporary difficulties had been foreseen for the immediate transitional stage, but these have generally been few. This has been due largely to the very considerable apprehensions which were entertained *before* the tax was introduced and which led to two important decisions: firstly, the need to evolve as simple a system as possible, consistent with other requirements, and secondly, the need to give wide and imaginative publicity to the administrative arrangements which would be required, so as to enable all those affected to understand what was expected of them. In addition, of course, the extent of the change in the tax structure was not as great as it would be in the UK, either because of the existence of similar or related systems of turnover tax, as in France and Germany, for example, or because of a more broadly based indirect tax system as in the case of Denmark and Luxembourg.

4.25 The main administrative problems arose from the fact that the number of taxpayers increases considerably with VAT covering all stages of production, wholesale, retail and services. Depending on the coverage of the tax systems already in force, the number of taxpayers—all of which have to be registered and assimilated into the system—increases two- or three-fold.

4.26 In order to reduce the number of entrepreneurs liable to tax, very small retailers and/or businesses with annual receipts ranging between £300 (in the case of Denmark) and £1,370 (in Germany) were exempted from VAT. This had the effect of reducing the number of taxpayers by up to one third. (In some countries this mainly administrative measure was given 'social' or 'small business' justifications.) However, although exempt themselves, the customers of these small businesses are nonetheless allowed a credit for tax passed on to them. In the Netherlands, certain farmers, livestock owners, horticulturists and foresters also do not pay VAT, as they are not considered as entrepreneurs (VAT Law Article 27 (i)) provided that their deliveries and services consist exclusively of certain specified items listed in the Law. These are essentially the items which are exported, and which have a preferential VAT rate on the home market. (The zero rate is not encouraged by the EEC Council's Second Directive but special arrangements are, in principle, possible for the agricultural community.) These farmers and other similar small businesses can opt to be classed as entrepreneurs, if they themselves wish to benefit from any tax credits due to them; whatever the choice it must be adhered to for five years.

4.27 In order to try to simplify collection and checking, small to medium sized enterprises with annual turnovers of limited specified amount, either must have (eg France) or could opt to have (eg Germany) their tax levied by an approximation to the accounts method instead of by the invoice method. In France where the turnover limit to qualify for this treatment is approximately £3,500, some 75 per cent of the enterprises are under this system. They are assessed at mid-term on a two-yearly basis, although if a major change develops in their situation their tax position can be adjusted. The inconvenience of this system is that the same firm's turnover may fluctuate around the limit: thus it sometimes falls under one set of administrative arrangements, sometimes under another. In Germany the annual turnover limit is £6,800, and enterprises were allowed to choose in advance whether they wished to be subject to the VAT invoice method or whether they preferred the old four per cent turnover tax (based on the former accounts method). The disadvantage of the latter is that when the firm's value added is not very high, no tax credits are allowed. Whatever the choice, it has to be adhered to for five years. There is evidence that several wrong options were made, and many businesses regretted their choice. The authorities themselves hope that this anomaly, which was added to the tax law at a late stage, will soon disappear. These attempts at simplification do not seem to have been very successful, though the number of enterprises affected is considerable, and the motives for adopting them were not economic but to relieve small shopkeepers from burdensome detailed accounting.

4.28 The taxable period varies considerably both with respect to countries and to categories of business. One month (the norm according to the Second EEC Council Directive) is the usual basis in France, Germany and the Netherlands. In Sweden it is every two months, and in Denmark quarterly returns are required. Very small businesses with low annual turnovers can report every quarter in most countries, while Sweden also allows half-yearly and yearly returns. In Denmark, where the agricultural community is of very great importance, farmers are allowed to pay VAT in two instalments; one half after five months and 20 days and the other half after eight months and 20 days. There had been some doubt about subjecting the agricultural community to VAT (and a suggestion to allow it a reduced rate), but the highly mechanised state of Danish farming made the tax credits so important that the farmers themselves chose to be included. Their produce is sold through co-operatives which have a very large export component. Their tax credits are repaid in about one week.

4.29 The refund of net tax credits is in theory supposed to be as rapid as possible. The main reason is to ensure the maintenance of business liquidity. These credits arise chiefly on exports, but also where there is a high proportion of tax exempt, or reduced rate sales, or a large ration of investment purchases to sales. All export credits are immediately refunded—even in France (see paragraph 4.30). For administrative reasons most countries only make actual refunds if there is either a constant credit and/or where the credit (ie tax invoiced on purchases less tax due on sales) is normally of a certain minimum amount. In Sweden, for instance, a steady monthly credit of a minimum of about £80 will allow a monthly return and a monthly refund. In Germany if the amount of the credit is a minimum of about £100, it is refunded; while in Denmark, apart from exports, refunds are paid after application. Normally smaller or irregular tax credits arising are carried over and deducted from the tax liability of the next return. In France the tax credits cannot be deducted immediately in the month in which they arise, but only in the following month.

4.30 The exception to this general practice of refunds of tax credits is France, where the 'buffer rule' in fact makes possible the accumulation of very large tax credits by businesses. There is, in France, no refund of net tax credits— except those arising from exports. This means that a firm investing heavily, for instance in the starting up phase, can accumulate very substantial net tax credits which, once their validity has been established, it has to carry over indefinitely until they are used up by offsetting liabilities. This is one cause for dissatisfaction with the French VAT system, among the business community. Both the non-refund and the one month's lag in tax credit utilisation (on investment credits however the lag is waived) are theoretically unjustified. The need for reform is generally acknowledged, but budget requirements have so far prevented it. This carrying forward of tax credit is also in fact an interest-free loan to the Government. It has been estimated that industry, ie excluding distribution and agriculture, advanced in 1968 some three billion francs to the French Government in this way.

4.31 Part of the tax credits arise because the purchases of tax-exempt capital goods take place sporadically. Each country seems to have its own regulations about tax credits for investment goods. Machinery, which according to the EEC Council's Second Directive should be credited for tax purposes over a five-year period, ie at an annual rate of 20 per cent, and buildings, are usually treated separately. The variance in practice affects the size of the tax credits arising. The treatment of investment goods will probably eventually have to be submitted to more far-reaching harmonisation in the Community.

4.32 While the exact administrative procedures in each country cannot be described in full, some of the more interesting aspects deserve to be mentioned. In Denmark and Sweden all payments must be made through the postal giro system. In Denmark a single office handles all the tax returns for the whole country. It is highly computerised, but can still share its computer capacity with other authorities.

4.33 In Germany the processes of collection and verification are separated, and this is considered to provide a very important simplification of administration procedures. The collection is done on the basis of monthly returns (self assessment) by aggregating tax liability on sales and tax credits on purchases. The collection of tax is done through the Länder Governments, ie it is not done centrally, though the VAT receipts are an essential part of the federal budget. The periodic verification, on the other hand, is carried out by the officials responsible for verifying profits for corporation (and income) tax. The unification of these two procedures is rational because essentially the same records and accounts are needed in both cases.

4.34 All countries rely on unheralded spot checks of sample invoices. These spot checks, which can be undertaken by junior staff, have proved to be very effective in maintaining invoicing standards, and in this way the self-checking mechanism of the VAT system is strengthened. Very large businesses in all countries are usually vetted yearly, though a period of between one and three years appears to be normal for most enterprises. Smaller businesses are visited less frequently, but the aim is to conduct a detailed examination of their accounts once in three to five years.

The costs of administration

4.35 The cost of administering the VAT system in the European countries is very difficult to assess. No country has introduced a VAT without abolishing or substantially modifying an existing indirect tax system. This may have been a single-stage wholesale tax, as in Denmark; or a retail sales tax, as in Sweden and Norway; a turnover tax, a services tax and a large number of special, low revenue excise taxes as in France; or a multi-stage cascade type turnover tax (as was the case in Belgium, Germany, the Netherlands and Luxembourg).

Many countries have also made simultaneous adjustments to their direct taxes (lowering them at least for small incomes), and often increased social benefits to non-taxpayers. Obviously, the staff formerly occupied in assessing, collecting and verifying the former taxation systems, are available to be used for the VAT. This is true, not only of the appropriate civil servants, but also of those in private business and commerce who were doing the necessary accounting work for the old taxes. It should be noted that, as a rule, only the complete abolition of a tax or, in the case of direct taxation especially, the reduction of the number of taxpayers, actually reduces staff requirements. The mere reduction of rates of tax does not have this effect.

4.36 It is, therefore, extremely difficult to estimate the net costs of collecting VAT. It is even difficult to obtain estimates of government staff involved in its collection and verification. In France a major programme of reform and streamlining of the tax system was introduced on 1 January 1970, involving total computerisation (in 10 separate tax divisions), simplification of documentation and the amalgamation of the three branches of the tax administration, leading to verification by one process. Previously, France had been the country with the most complicated VAT system, and the least streamlined method of collection. In spite of this the extension of VAT to the retail stage in 1968 did not require a general increase in customs and excise staff because staff economies were possible, due to the abolition of other taxes, which were mainly special taxes yielding small sums of revenue and having high administrative costs. Since the reforms of 1970, the composition of this complement of about 11,000 civil servants has been altered so that more than half are junior staff and less than half more senior administrators.

4.37 In Germany widely differing estimates were given about the number of tax officials required to administer the tax, ranging from 3,000 to 8,000. The latter figure is the more plausible in relation to estimates which have been made for the UK, and the smaller one could refer either to the number of senior staff, or perhaps the number which might have been possible if a single rate of tax had been adopted (see paragraph 4.38).

4.38 So far as the governments are concerned, a combination of several factors has enabled staff and costs to be contained. These consist of switching available staff, using modern mechanised account and payment systems (Denmark and Sweden have all payments made through the postal giro), and making the documentation as simple as possible. As an illustration, both the Danish (very simple) and the French (less simple) forms are appended to this chapter.

4.39 Having more than a single VAT rate has been estimated to increase the governments' administrative costs by 50–80 per cent. That multiple rates must also increase costs correspondingly for business enterprises is obvious, but no estimates are available.

4.40 It seems that the large and medium sized firms which had computer systems, or machine accounting, found that even a multi-rate system of VAT was relatively easy to cope with. There have been few complaints about any additional costs, and few of other administrative problems. Where these have arisen, they have come mainly from the, sometimes not very simple, transitional regulations, especially those connected with the treatment of stocks and investment goods.

4.41 These judgements applied also to many of the firms where accounting was still done manually. One by-product of the introduction of VAT has been a boom in the sales of the simpler mechanical calculating machines. While no firm evidence can exist, it seems that the introduction of VAT has forced a mechanisation of accounting procedures in many firms. The economies resulting from mechanising and rationalising accounting, can to some extent offset the time that has to be spent on administering VAT. (A survey in Germany of a number of businesses showed that they estimated that the extra administrative work *on taxation* caused by the introduction of VAT varied between about five and twenty per cent. As this survey was made soon after the changeover to VAT, it may overestimate the real long term costs.)

4.42 The real problem arises in those enterprises, particularly the small firms, which have never appreciated the importance of proper accounting: where these firms were either exempted from VAT or subject to assessment by the accounts method, they were in fact also more or less absolved from improving their accounting methods. According to the Second Directive of the EEC Council, enterprises are normally under an obligation to keep suitable accounts.

4.43 The two main transitional periods during which abnormally high administrative costs are liable to arise, both for the revenue authorities and for business, are first, in the period of introduction of a VAT when there are difficulties associated with the immediate impact of a new tax, falling on new goods, and collected in new ways, and this tends to last for about six to twelve months, depending on the complexity of the system of tax accounting and the success of the preliminary campaign of education and publicity. The second period of difficulty is likely to last a good deal longer, perhaps up to five years, during which special transitional devices have to be employed to overcome the frictions and anomalies arising from the removal of one tax system and the introduction of another. While the variations in the individual countries are as complex and differentiated as those of VAT itself, an important transitional problem is that capital equipment and stocks, on which previous taxes have already been paid, should not be subject to double taxation on the introduction of the VAT. The transitional difficulties which have undoubtedly existed, though their importance has varied greatly in various countries, have mainly, but not exclusively, been confined so far to the initial impact stage. The doubts entertained as to the possible adverse effect which the introduction of VAT could have on business liquidity also proved to be exaggerated—such effects, if any, were of short duration.

Other tax changes 4.44 The introduction of VAT has usually been accompanied by other tax changes. As it is, in fact, a broadly based tax on consumption, capable of greatly increasing the revenue from indirect taxation it is almost inevitable that some consequential adjustments in other taxes would have to be made.

4.45 The introduction of VAT can provide the opportunity for a major restructuring of taxation. This opportunity was taken in Denmark, where VAT was introduced at the same time as a PAYE system. The opportunity was taken to alter the rates of direct taxation, especially to reduce them for smaller incomes and to give increased allowances to those below the taxation threshold, and also to abolish the wholesale, single-stage, tax. Similar changes were made in Norway.

4.46 The introduction of VAT has also led to adjustments of the rates of indirect taxation on so called luxury items, though the degree to which this has been done has varied greatly. In France and Germany VAT rates were chosen so that the change should be broadly 'neutral', ie so that the maximum rates in force before the introduction of VAT were not increased. In practice, this meant that in France all items defined as luxuries are subject to the highest VAT rate. Many items classified as luxuries in other countries, and these include watches, perfumes, toiletries, beauty care, caviar and some furs and skins, are taxed at the standard rate. In Germany the old cascade turnover tax was completely replaced by the two-rate VAT. This meant that all prices had to be recalculated. An evaluation of the overall readjustments which this required is probably impossible as, in some cases where the introduction of VAT would have meant a rise in price, the increases were partly absorbed by the manufacturers due to market price resistance. As a general principle, distributors' *net* margins were left unchanged by the producers when recalculating retail prices. There are still some excise taxes in Germany other than VAT, but their rates were apparently reduced so so that when VAT was added, total taxation did not increase. In the Netherlands the duty on tobacco was maintained, that on alcohol was raised by 10 per cent and a 'special consumption tax' of 15 per cent was imposed on deliveries and imports of passenger cars. The aim of this was to keep the rates at which these items are taxed at approximately the same levels as those which obtained under the former turnover tax. These special taxes and any luxury and/or excise taxes are included in the tax base for VAT.

4.47 In Denmark, Norway and Sweden the single rate of VAT was, in general, added to the already high excise duties on so called luxury items. In Denmark, a minor concession was made by reductions of excise duties on radio and television sets and cigars and, when the VAT rate was raised from 10 to 12½ per cent, also on alcohol served in restaurants. On all other 'luxury' products, including tobacco, oil, alcohol, confectionery, ice-cream, gramophones, jewellery, watches and cosmetics, VAT is calculated on a basis tax-inclusive of the high excise duties already levied.

4.48 In several countries, though not in France, discussions are in progress about eventually raising the rates of VAT in order to make possible alterations in the proportions of 'direct' and 'indirect' taxation. This is partly due to the tax harmonisation intentions of the EEC, but is also based on domestic (political, social and economic) considerations. It is fairly widely expected that, sometime in the 1970's a move will be made towards a more even balance between direct and indirect taxes—and that the harmonisation of taxes will lead to a general change in all rates including those of VAT.

VAT as a source of revenue

4.49 One of the main reasons why VAT has been or is being introduced is that it can be a very buoyant source of revenue. Most countries have, to varying degrees, had purchase taxes on luxury items at such a level that any further increase might lead to a reduction of revenue. By including the retail and services sectors in VAT the tax base is very widely increased, and this allows substantial revenues to be raised at relatively moderate rates.

4.50 In Denmark and the Netherlands VAT provides about one-fifth of total tax revenue, in Germany it is about one-quarter, while in France and Norway the proportion is around 40 per cent.

The effect on prices

4.51 It is only in the six countries which have had VAT at the retail stage for a year or longer that it is possible to estimate the effect of its introduction on prices. These seem generally to have been less than was expected, although there are exceptions. Naturally, efforts were made, either through lower rates or exemptions, by the simultaneous removal of other taxes and a careful and sustained programme of advance publicity in the press, on TV and radio, and through pamphlets and brochures, to educate the public about the mechanism of the new tax and to minimise its effects on incomes and prices. It is not, of course, possible to draw firm conclusions as to what might happen in the UK in this respect because the final price effect would depend entirely on what decisions were taken with regard to existing taxes and what other pressures were felt on costs.

4.52   In Germany both sides of industry are in agreement that no general price increase due to VAT seems to have occurred. Some goods, such as tinned foods and textiles benefited and became cheaper; certain services, such as haircuts, restaurant meals and laundries, with a high value added element, showed the largest price increases. Formerly taxed at 4 per cent, they now had to pay eleven per cent. The overall price increase of 0·9 per cent in Germany in the six months up to July 1968 is believed to have had little to do with the introduction of VAT.

4.53   In France the price increase in the three months January to March 1968, following the introduction of the VAT, was only 1·15 per cent, and probably not all of this increase was due to VAT.

4.54   In Denmark, on the other hand, the country whose situation is closest to that of the UK, the cost of living rose by 7·9 per cent in the first six months after the introduction of VAT, due mainly to VAT being levied on food, and also for the first time on services. The rise had been expected, and it did not lead to any serious discontent, largely because there had been some very substantial wage increases shortly before the introduction of the VAT, and it was also accompanied by tax concessions for lower incomes and increased allowances for non-taxed persons. Thus the impact of the price changes was mitigated.

4.55   In the Netherlands, where the tax became effective at the beginning of 1969, there was also a sharp increase in prices of over 5 per cent in the first three months. A general price freeze was introduced on 1 April 1969, and replaced on 4 September by a 'calculation rule', which allowed merchants and manufacturers to pass on certain external cost increases in their prices. The measures taken succeeded in keeping the cost of living increase over the year to 6 per cent. Only about 1·5 per cent of the increase was thought to be directly attributable to the VAT; it is widely believed that its introduction triggered off the increases, and provided traders with the opportunity for an upward adjustment of margins which had been under pressure for several years. Both Norway and Luxembourg applied a price freeze when introducing VAT. In Norway the freeze straddled the introduction of VAT. In spite of this, retail prices rose by 6·25 per cent between the last quarter of 1969 and the first quarter of 1970; a 5·8 per cent increase had been calculated as the probable effect of the introduction of VAT. In Luxembourg, where VAT exactly replaced a multi-stage turnover tax up to retail stage and including services, no effect on the general level of prices was expected. A price freeze was, however, imposed from January to June, during which time retail prices rose by just over 2 per cent.

Attitudes of governments, industry and trade unions

4.56 EEC governments introduced VAT because of the agreed policy as set out in the Council's First and Second Directives, and also as a step to the eventual harmonisation of all indirect taxes on a country of origin basis, implying in the future that there would be uniform multi-stage taxes on all value added within the Community. However, without the outside pressure of the Directives it would probably not have been possible because of general inertia and conflicting political interests, to obtain the tax reform. The countries outside the EEC (Denmark, Sweden and now Norway) say that they introduced VAT because they considered it a more satisfactory tax than those they had before, because the Nordic Council of Scandinavian countries suggested in 1964 that they too should consider introducing VAT, and also of course because they are candidates for EEC membership.

4.57 The reasons which have been given by governments for favouring VAT are mainly the following:

a VAT allows in theory, and may make possible in practice, uniform customs and excise at frontiers and the eventual adoption of a country of origin basis for all indirect taxes.

b VAT is, in some senses, a neutral form of taxation. Its imposition should not seriously distort the allocation of resources or the industrial structure, because it should be borne by the consumer and not by production units. (Exemptions and differential rates must be kept reasonably small if this characteristic of VAT is to be achieved.)

c VAT is a good revenue raiser. Because of the extension of indirect taxation to almost all consumer items, including services and distribution, comparatively low rates of taxation can bring in very considerable funds. This is the case even when compensation is made to lower income groups through reductions in direct taxation or increased allowances.

d In common with other taxes on consumption, VAT tends to favour savings.

e As producer goods under VAT benefit from total tax exemption, VAT should encourage investment, if capital goods were previously subject to tax.

4.58 In all countries having a VAT, the management side of industry generally regards the tax favourably, because it provides the Exchequer with an alternative to higher rates of direct tax on corporate and business income, an alternative which they regard as having less disincentive effects so far as effort, risk-taking and investment are concerned. The introduction of a VAT was seen by most business men, however, as a considerable improvement on the forms of indirect taxation which had existed previously in their countries, although even now many anomalies and special problems still exist and produce familiar complaints.

4.59 Many trade union organisations in Europe have tended to see the positive sides of VAT, and have given it a cautious welcome. Again it is the comparison with previous taxation arrangements which has been primarily responsible for influencing their views. They are usually adamant, however, that essential goods and services should not be taxed at rates higher than before. This is a major reason for the adoption of multiple rates of VAT in the EEC countries. It is significant that in the three Scandinavian countries, which have a high average standard of living, and where tax and social security compensations were made for the lowest incomes, a single rate of VAT was introduced.

4.60 Finally, governments, businessmen and trade unions, as well as tax experts, are of the opinion that, when VAT is kept as simple as possible, preferably with a single rate, the administrative problems and cost at both the government and at the enterprise level can be contained.

4.61 For the future, the balance between VAT and other forms of taxation will probably depend on the political, social and economic requirements of the countries involved. How it will evolve in the EEC, when the whole structure of taxation is due for harmonisation, is an open question, but so far as VAT is concerned, it may be possible to progress towards the elimination or reduction of multiple rates, and the simplification of the many present exemptions and special regulations.

Annex
VAT documentation
in Europe

4.62 Among the administrative problems posed by a VAT, the kind of documentation and form filling procedures which would be required naturally loom very large in the minds of businessmen. Obviously the precise shape, layout and content of the forms which might be adopted in the UK cannot be foreseen, but as an indication of what might be involved we have made facsimile translations into English of the forms employed by the Danish and French authorities.

4.63 The Danish documents are extremely simple, largely because the tax is levied at a single rate with few exemptions. The first form, Illustration 1, is a record of transactions which is maintained by the businessman and trader in a special accounting booklet issued by the Directorate of Taxes. It shows his purchases and the tax credits arising from them, and it shows his sales and the tax payments for which he is liable. Provided his own existing accounting allows the details required to be identified, the businessman need not alter his own accounting method. Should the existing accounting be deficient or non-existent, then records must be kept as specified in the form shown in Illustration 1. (In fact, although this accounting layout was originally evolved for the small firm it is in general use.) At the end of the tax period he totals up these credits and liabilities and enters them on the form in Illustration 2, which is sent to the tax authorities.

Illustration 1 DANISH VAT FORM

Value Added Tax
TAX ACCOUNTING

Date	Purchases				Sales			Comments
	1 Purchase price including VAT	Tax Credit			4 Sales price	5 Tax payable	6 VAT deductible on exports	
		2 Domestic purchases	3 on own imports					

Illustration 2

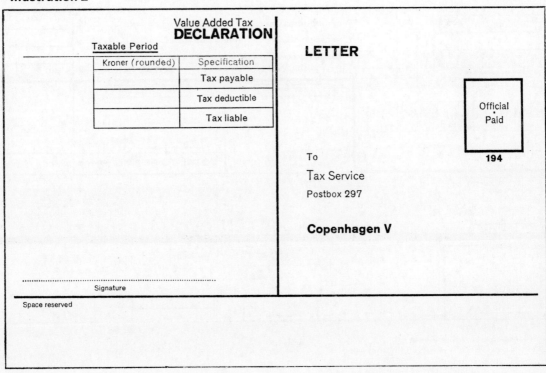

Value Added Tax
DECLARATION

Taxable Period

Kroner (rounded)	Specification
	Tax payable
	Tax deductible
	Tax liable

....
Signature

Space reserved

LETTER

Official
Paid

194

To

Tax Service

Postbox 297

Copenhagen V

Illustration 3 FRENCH VAT FORM

No. 3310M

C A 3

DIRECTORATE OF TAXES

TURNOVER TAXES

AND ASSIMILATED TAXES

IDENTIFICATION NO. OF THE ENTERPRISE

IDENTIFICATION no. of establishment making the return

RETURN FOR THE MONTH OF ⬚ OR THE ⬚ QUARTER 19

A (I) **TAX ON VALUE ADDED:** Write on lines 01 to 10 below and in the columns corresponding to the appropriate rate of VAT the amount, including tax, attributable to transactions concluded during the tax period. **Give totals for the columns in the spaces a, b, c and d, rounded up to the nearest franc.**

■ TRANSACTIONS LIABLE TO VAT	REDUCED RATE 1	INTERMEDIATE RATE 2	STANDARD RATE 3	HIGHER RATE 4	LINE TOTALS 5	
01 Sale of purchased goods without further processing						01
02 Sale of products manufactured by the enterprise...						02
03 Sale for immediate consumption.....................						03
04 Services supplied						04
05 Provision of accommodation..........						05
06 Building work.............						06
07						07
08 Transactions partially liable to tax ⎱ AMOUNT LIABLE						08
09 Deliveries to self................						
10 Purchases from non-taxpayers.........						Total for lines 01–08 col. 5 to be carried forward overleaf Section B line 37
11 **TOTAL** (col. 5)...................						11

■ CALCULATION of the TAX

	no	codes							F C
	12*	0100	a					6%	
Apply to each of the tax bases obtained in spaces a, b, c and d the appropriate rate of VAT.	13*	0200		b				13%	
The amount of VAT at the rate of 16⅔% can be obtained by dividing the tax base at c by 6, rather than multiplying by the approximate rate of 16.66%.	14*	0300			c			16⅔%	
Write the results in francs and centimes on lines 12–15 column 5.	15*	0400				d		20%	
	16*								
	17*	0900	Previous rates of VAT..............						
	18*	0600	VAT deducted earlier to be carried forward ⎰ in respect of capital assets..............						
	19*	0610	in respect of other goods and services....						
	20		● **GROSS VAT** (total of lines 12–19) ────────➤						
■ Calculate VAT deductible overleaf, Section C	21*	0700	● **VAT DEDUCTIBLE** (calculated overleaf, Section C) ──➤						
	22		● **NET VAT** (difference line 20 — line 21) ──────➤						
■ Calculate other taxes overleaf, Section D	23	(1)	(II) **OTHER TAXES** (total given overleaf, Section D, line 67) ──➤						
(1) Leave this space blank	24		(Line 22 + Line 23) **TOTAL TAX** ────➤						

■ Mark with cross the box showing the method of payment:

1 CASH	2 CHEQUE	3 GIRO TRANSFER	4 STATE BOND	5

RECEIVED	PENALTY FOR ARREARS	
Sum	State............	9000.........
Date	Rate ....%	Others...........
No.		
No. 3853–44a	**TOTAL TO BE PAID ➤**	

Place ....Signature.............

Date...............

DEPARTMENT OF INDIRECT TAXATION

Giro account

This return must be made to the department named opposite.

Date of receipt

Local Authority	Offices	Receipt	No. of file	Key	Period	Activity	S	System

ADDRESS OF THE ESTABLISHMENT

(where this differs from the addressee's) ➤

C.E.R.F.A. No. 30-0469

B DETAILS OF TRANSACTIONS CONCLUDED DURING THE TAX PERIOD

Sum rounded up to the nearest franc

Most Important

This section must be completed by all taxpayers.
If you have made no transactions in any individual category, write the figure 0 on the appropriate line.

31* Exports..
32* Transactions assimilated to exports..
33* Sales under suspension of tax..
34* Transactions partially liable to tax: NON-TAXABLE AMOUNT....................
35* Other tax-free transactions..

• 36 Total tax-free transactions (total of lines 31–35)........................
• 37 Total taxable transactions (brought forward from line 11, col. 5 of Section A)........

38* ■ TOTAL TRANSACTIONS (line 36 · line 37).............................➤   F

CAPITAL ASSETS, acquired during the tax period.

39* Value of assets eligible for deduction (exclusive of VAT deducted at line b, Section C)........
40* Value of assets not eligible for deduction (incl. VAT)......................

C CALCULATION OF VAT DEDUCTIBLE (VAT on purchases, imports etc.)

(Sums expressed in francs and centimes)
F   C

• a Credit appearing at line 5, Section C of previous return

attributable to CAPITAL ASSETS

b VAT on ASSETS acquired during the tax period (I)............................
c VAT not mentioned on previous returns (I)...................................
d Balance of VAT for deduction (annual adjustment) ....
e Transfers of entitlement to deduction......................................

• f Total of lines b to e...................................➤ 46*

(I) allowing for the DEDUCTION PERCENTAGE applicable to the enterprise.
▼
................%

attributable to OTHER GOODS and SERVICES

g VAT on GOODS and SERVICES acquired during previous month (2)................
h VAT not mentioned on previous returns......................................
I VAT deductible in respect of stocks at 31.12.67 (utilisable portion).......
j

• k Total of lines g to j..................................➤ 48*

m ■ TOTAL VAT DEDUCTIBLE (total of lines a, f and k)..................➤

(2) or acquired during the 3 months preceding the last month of the quarter for which return is made

Compare the total VAT deductible (line m above) with the total gross VAT (line 20 of Section A, p.1)
➤ **WRITE THE SMALLER OF THESE TWO SUMS ON LINE 21 OF SECTION A** ◄
CALCULATE THE NET VAT TO BE PAID (line 22 of Section A). Where this amount is NIL (i.e. where full allowance for VAT deductible cannot be charged) fill in lines p to s below.

Utilisation of credit not entered on present return

p VAT deductible not entered on the present return (difference: line m of Section C – line 20 of Section A)........
q VAT deductible transferred to other enterprises............................
r Refund applied for...
s **CREDIT CARRIED FORWARD** to line a of Section C of next return (difference: line p — lines q and r)........

D CALCULATION OF OTHER TAXES

		– 1 –	Amount of transactions liable to tax, – 2 – F	Gross tax – 3 – F C	Tax deductible – 4 – F C	Net Tax payable – 5 – F C
51*	◆	Special tax on financial activities....................13%				
52*	3100	Taxes on { National Forestry Fund.............3.50%				
53*	3210	forest products { BAPSA 1.00%				
54*	3400	Contribution: Clothing technical centre..........0.50%				
55*	3600	Contribution: Dyeing and cleaning technical centre........1%				
56*	4000	Tax on textiles.................................0.35%				
57*	3900	Tax: Professional committee for horology........0.70%				
58*	3700	Contribution: Leather technical centre...........0.40%				
59*	3500	Contribution: National fund for publishing.......0.20%				
60*	3220	Tax on sugar beet..............................8.50%				
61*						
62*	1001	Taxes abolished from 1st January 1968 { Tax on services supplied: 8.50%......				
63*	1002	Local tax: 2.75%				
64*	1003	Local tax: 8.50%				
65*		%.				
66*	1000		x x x x x x x x	Total lines 62–65 (col. 3) ➤		
67		Total of lines 51–61 (col. 5) + line 66 (col. 5) ■ TOTAL OTHER TAXES carried forward to line 23 Section A ➤				

4.64 The French document, of which Illustration 3 is a translation, shows the much greater complexity which arises from a system having four rates of tax and a wide range of exemptions and supplementary taxes. Businessmen and traders are under obligation to keep exactly corresponding accounts for record and inspection purposes.

(*Note:* The VAT rates shown in Illustration 3, are those which were in force up to November 1968. They have since been increased.)

A value added tax in the UK 5

5.1 As has been suggested earlier, the introduction of a VAT in the UK would involve major social, economic and administrative policy decisions which cannot be anticipated, and which can only be discussed on a tentative and hypothetical basis. It is possible, however, to draw attention to some of the major issues which would be involved, and on which these necessary decisions would have to be taken.

5.2 Clearly, among the most important of these decisions would be the rate or rates of tax which would be imposed, its general coverage, and what the implications for tax revenue as a whole might be. Secondly, there are the administrative arrangements which might be adopted, and the question of how some of the widely recognised problems which might arise in this field could be overcome. Thirdly, there are the implications which would follow from different kinds of tax changes which might be made as a result of the adoption of a VAT; among the many possibilities here are the replacement of a part of corporate direct taxation, and/or the restructuring of indirect taxation. Finally, there is the question of whether certain of the objectives of a VAT could not be achieved in some other, and perhaps better way.

Rates and coverage of a VAT*

5.3 Detailed consideration of the possible rate or rates at which a VAT might be introduced in the UK, and the coverage of various items, cannot be given in advance of certain prior decisions being made with regard to revenue requirements, which other taxes were to be modified, and which other social and economic objectives were being pursued. Nevertheless, it is necessary to have some broad indication of the orders of magnitude and the general considerations which have to be taken into account.

5.4 There are two preliminary considerations which should be borne in mind: one is the experience and practice of other countries, and the other is the primary requirement of any tax that it should produce sufficient public revenue. It is sometimes popularly supposed that a VAT can be levied widely at a very low, almost imperceptible, rate of 2–3 per cent, thus providing that long sought after ideal, painless taxation. This is a misapprehension which arises primarily from confusion with the cumulative turnover taxes which have previously existed in some European countries, and in which very low nominal rates, levied at a series of stages, amounted to a considerable tax burden on final sales. It has already been shown in Chapter 4 that, under contemporary VAT arrangements in Europe, the 'basic' rate of tax lies in the 11–20 per cent range (23 per cent in France).

5.5 The second consideration is that the rate or rates of VAT must be related to the amounts of revenue which are required to be raised. The size and structure of UK tax revenue currently being raised from existing taxes was shown in Chapter 3, but may be summarised in Table 12.

* *The Note at the beginning of Chapter 3 is particularly relevant to the discussion of the possible rates and yields of a VAT.*

Table 12 Yields from existing taxes (1970/71 estimate)

	£ million
Income tax	5,653
Corporation tax	1,900
Tobacco, drink, oil	3,445
Purchase tax	1,260
SET (net)	588*
Motor vehicle duties	431
Other	851
Total tax revenue	£14,128

* net yield from private sector and public corporations.

Source: Financial Statement 1970/71.

5.6 In very round terms, as a first approximation and making no allowance
for the fact that in practice it is never possible to collect 100 per cent of the
theoretical yield, a VAT in the UK, covering all items of consumer spending
(net of existing taxes), and levied at a flat rate of 10 per cent would raise
about £2,200 million a year in revenue at 1969 prices, ie say about
£220 million for each 1 per cent of tax. Taxation on consumers'
expenditure in 1969 totalled about £5,000 million (tobacco, drink, and
consumers' share of oil duties, purchase tax, etc), so that a single rate of
VAT even if applied to all purchases, right across the board, would need
to be imposed at around 23 per cent in order to replace the whole of
existing revenue from consumption taxes. Clearly, if certain categories of
expenditure were to be exempted from the VAT for social, administrative
or economic reasons, the revenue yield would be reduced for a given basic
rate of VAT, or alternatively higher rates would have to be introduced to
maintain any given yield. The same consideration would apply if reduced,
preferential, rates were introduced on certain types of expenditure, and of
course similarly, but in the opposite direction, if sumptuary rates were
applied to luxury categories.

5.7 In view of this, one preliminary consideration which arises is whether a
VAT in the UK might be levied at a single rate across the board on
transactions in all goods and services, or whether a multi-rate system should
be adopted. In both cases this would include the question of what, if any,
exemptions might be applied. From many points of view, of course, a
single rate of tax has obvious advantages: it is administratively more simple,
it is easily understood and identified, and its incidence is neutral as between
one category of expenditure and another. But, in this sense, 'neutrality' is
not necessarily an unqualified virtue, for taxation may be required to
perform other functions such as the reinforcement of social attitudes and
priorities, and the bringing of social and private costs and returns more
closely into line. Thus while it may be iniquitous to tax the photographic
enthusiast heavily and exempt the yachtsman, it might be regarded as

equally perverse to tax the loaf and the mink alike. The fact is that, in contemplating any reform of the tax system, full regard must be paid to the characteristics of the existing tax structure and to the social, political and economic forces which have made it what it is. The diversity of practice which still exists in Europe is eloquent witness to the need for this (and, indeed, their adoption of the VAT itself was not such a revolutionary departure from existing tax systems as it would be in the UK).

5.8 The principle of differential, selective, indirect taxation is very firmly established and widely accepted in the UK, and would without doubt have to be retained to a very considerable extent. There are a number of ways in which this selectivity might be retained in a system which included a VAT:

a A single rate VAT could be introduced with differentials being provided by other taxes, such as the retention of all or part of purchase tax, or the excise duties on tobacco, drink etc

b A multiple rate VAT could be devised so as to supply all the desired differentials

c A multiple rate VAT could supply some of the selectivity, while other taxes supplied the remainder.

The first possibility would require the retention of so much of existing tax arrangements (even though rates might be adjusted) that the VAT would be simply an additional tax. The second would require an extremely complicated rate structure (with an attendant multiplication of administrative difficulties) unless the degree of selectivity were to be very substantially curtailed from what it is at present. Some variant of the third alternative seems, therefore, to be the most realistic prospect for any practicable system in the foreseeable future.

5.9 One element of selectivity in a single rate system of VAT could be provided by means of exemptions or zero rates, although the scope for this would necessarily be limited. For purely illustrative purposes, and in order to estimate the possible yields of a VAT and the impact which it might have on the distribution of incomes, two possible schemes of rates and coverage may be considered. The first is a simple and comprehensive scheme, closest perhaps to the Danish arrangements, while the second possibility retains more selectivity:

Scheme A: A single VAT rate of 10 per cent on all transactions, except for foodstuffs which would be exempted, and assuming no effective change in the total revenue derived from tobacco, drink and hydrocarbon oils.

Scheme B: A basic rate of $12\frac{1}{2}$ per cent, with a higher rate of 25 per cent on all goods now bearing purchase tax at a rate above the lowest rate, but exempting:

a Food

b Rent, rates, water charges, vehicle licences

c Fuel and light

d Books, newspapers and magazines

e Travel by rail, bus, coach, etc

and assuming no effective net change in the revenue from tobacco, alcohol and hydrocarbon oils.

5.10 If a VAT were introduced a decision would have to be taken on what would happen to existing taxes on goods and services, and in particular to the excise duties on tobacco, alcohol, and hydrocarbon oils. So far as the purchase tax is concerned it is assumed for the purposes of this illustration, that it would be wholly replaced, except possibly under the 'simple' regime for the retention of one supplementary luxury rate on a small number of specified products. (If this were not done the abrupt change in relative prices could have harmful effects.) It should be noted, however, that the retention of any part of an existing tax would greatly reduce any administrative economies which might be possible. The heavy excise duties present a somewhat different problem; they exist at their present level for a complex of social, historical and political reasons and it is scarcely

Table 13 Yield of VAT on 1967 consumption data (£'000 million)

Scheme A		
Consumers' expenditure in UK		25·0
Less: Expenditure on food, drink, tobacco and petrol	9·8	
Yield of purchase tax	0·7	
	10·5	−10·5
Tax base		14·5

VAT yield at 10 per cent = £1,450 million, plus an estimated £150 million arising from the non-recovery of tax levied on inputs into food and agriculture.

Total theoretical yield = about £1,600 million.

Scheme B		
Consumers' expenditure (as above)		25·0
Less: Value of higher purchase tax goods	2·2	
Expenditure on food, drink, tobacco, petrol, rent, rates, water, fuel and light, books, travel etc	14·3	
Residual purchase tax on other goods	0·2	
	16·7	−16·7
Expenditure liable to VAT at 12½ per cent		8·3
Expenditure liable to VAT at 25 per cent		1·8
Yield from 12½ per cent rate	1·0	
Yield from 25 per cent rate	0·5	
Plus non-recovery of tax on exempted items	0·4	

Total theoretical yield = about £1,900 million.

conceivable that they could disappear, even under the more 'realistic' regime outlined above. It is more likely that the excise duty could be reduced to take account of the new VAT element in the price, leaving the total tax element unchanged, and this is the assumption which has been used in these two illustrative schemes, which are shown in Table 13. The illustrations are based upon 1967 consumption and tax data.

5.11 Estimates of this kind are inevitably very approximate, and can do no more than illustrate broad orders of magnitude without taking account of any shifts in consumption patterns which might arise, or of the practical consideration that it is not possible to collect 100 per cent of the theoretical yield. Moreover, in addition to the specified exemptions noted above there are various types of consumer expenditure which would inevitably fall outside the tax net on social, cultural or de minimis grounds. It is impossible to say accurately what these might amount to in terms of lost revenue but we would put it prudently at about £200 million. Thus the actual tax yield on the assumptions we have used would probably be of the order of about £1,400 million in Scheme A and £1,700 million in Scheme B, based on 1967 tax data.

5.12 Of course, these sums do not represent a net increase in revenue from the Government's point of view, or a net increase in the tax burden so far as the consumer is concerned. It has already been assumed that purchase tax would disappear, and with a VAT extending over the services sector SET would also be replaced. Thus, the net gain in tax revenue at these rates which could be used to finance other existing taxation is of the order of about £250 million–£400 million (based on 1967 tax data).

5.13 It is estimated that the effect of a VAT at these rates and coverage, if replacing purchase tax alone would increase the cost of living index by about $2\frac{1}{2}$–3 per cent, and if SET also disappeared the effect would be between $1\frac{1}{2}$ and 2 per cent.

5.14 It is possible that these yields would provide insufficient revenue to undertake any further tax switching on a significant scale. If in Scheme A the rate was raised to $12\frac{1}{2}$ per cent the theoretical yield would rise to about £2,000 million. In Scheme B if higher rates of, say 15 per cent and 25 per cent were adopted the theoretical yield would be nearer £2,200 million.

The administration of a VAT

5.15 There are very broadly two ways in which a VAT could be introduced and which have been described in Chapter 2; these are the 'accounts' method, and the 'invoicing' or 'tax-from-tax' method. The latter is being generally adopted in the EEC and Scandinavia and it requires the invoicing of the VAT on the bill of sale on every transaction up to the stage of sales to final consumers, in order to charge the seller VAT on the value of his total domestic sales, and also to enable him to be credited with the tax already invoiced to him on his purchases. An important advantage of this method is that it allows the possibility of VAT being levied at different rates on value added arising in the production of different commodities or at different stages of production.

5.16 The alternative method, the sales less purchases or accounts method, is to assess—at perhaps quarterly, six-monthly, or even annual intervals in arrears—the difference between the total sales of each business unit (excluding its export sales) and its total purchases (including purchases of capital) from other UK businesses. VAT is then assessed on this difference. One apparent advantage of this method of assessment is that it would seem to operate more like a direct business tax, though to the extent that it did appear in this light it might raise international difficulties in relation to rebating it on exports. Moreover, it would be difficult to operate differential rates of VAT side by side without identifying the actual commodities involved in individual sales and purchases (see Chapter 2 paragraphs 2.22–2.24).

Perhaps the most fundamental administrative objection which has been represented by the Inland Revenue against the accounts based system is that it would be out of the question to expect the business world, the accountancy profession, or the Revenue, to cope with the submission of even quarterly accounts, however limited they might be in scope*. An alternative would be to place on the trader the obligation to make an estimated calculation of his liability, quarter by quarter or month by month, and to make provisional payments of these sums. The Inland Revenue say, however, that self assessing on this scale would be a novelty in this country, and that it would be a long time before traders became accustomed to it and worked it successfully. Finally, the accounts method does not conform with the requirements of the EEC directives.

5.17 Therefore, although the accounts method appears to have the attraction of simplicity it does not seem to be a practical option at present, first, because no other country having a VAT has adopted it; and second, because ordinary summary business accounts do not lend themselves to the assessment of value added in the sense used in a VAT: special accounts would, therefore, be required, thus adding to the administrative burden on industry. If therefore a VAT were to be introduced into the UK it would probably be based on the invoicing system, and along lines similar to those existing in Europe.

5.18 The main administrative requirements of such a VAT would depend on the decisions which were taken relating to revenue requirements, the rate or rates at which the tax would be levied, and its broad coverage. Having

* *This latter objection to self assessment could also be taken to apply to an invoice-based system.*

reached these, the main issues which would have to be determined in legislation are:

a Definition of the taxable goods and services and exempt categories, including the basis on which VAT credits could be claimed.

b Definition of the taxable enterprises and the procedure for registration. This would raise problems relating to mixed enterprises, subsidiaries, and any special categories such as charities, trusts, public bodies, and so on.

c Definition of taxable value. In general it would be assumed that taxable value would be represented by the purchase price involved in the transaction, but some of the issues which would arise here would relate to rentals and hire purchase transactions, the treatment of discounts, and the timing of deliveries and payments. (It has also been noted in Chapter 4, however, that the taxable value in certain cases need not be 100 per cent of the purchase price).

d Determination of the form of accounts. A standardised form of accounting would be required, indicating all sales and purchases and the tax liabilities and credits for all transactions between taxable enterprises.

e Procedure for payment or reimbursement of net credits and liabilities. This would need to cover such questions as the frequency of payments and method of settlement.

f Procedures for inspection, control and verification.

5.19 There is a widespread feeling that such a VAT would be complicated and costly to administer, principally because of its comprehensiveness in the coverage of goods and services, and the very large number of traders (up to about two million) who would be brought within the tax net. Both of the revenue departments, the Inland Revenue and HM Customs and Excise, have indicated that they can foresee major new administrative problems arising if a VAT were to be introduced.

5.20 It is, first of all, the case that the historical background to the development of the fiscal system in the UK is different from that in European countries where the VAT has been adopted. Most of these countries have had a more broadly based indirect tax system or cumulative turnover taxes for several years, and this made easier the adoption of a VAT. Also, the introduction of a new comprehensive tax on goods and services in the UK would involve a massive programme of education, induction into the system, the organisation of documentation and procedures for handling millions of returns, and for the collection of the tax. Moreover, the greater the selectivity of the system, and/or the greater the number of exemptions, the greater would be the complications associated with borderline cases, definitions, multiple products, and so on. Even when the transitional difficulties had been overcome there would be the continuing problem of collection, verification and inspection from some two million taxable enterprises if the system were extended to the retail stage. Substantial increases in staff would be required by the revenue departments in order to maintain a tolerable degree of control: they have suggested that an overall increase of 4,000–5,000 would be needed to administer even an annual accounts-based value added tax, and that a far greater number of about 7,000 would be needed to administer an invoice-based system even if it initially extended only as far as the wholesale stage. The recruitment, training and organisation of good quality staff, of which there is already a severe shortage, would give rise to additional costs and difficulties. The administrative load and costs would not be confined to the Government, because for industry, special records would need to be maintained covering all transactions liable to or exempt from the tax. Finally a number of special problems would arise with small businesses, which at present keep no accounts or only very primitive ones. Here too, there would be problems of definition relating to the determination of what constituted a small business, and to the fact that such a definition would inevitably be arbitrary and sometimes anomalous. Similar difficulties could arise with certain special categories of business such as financial concerns, whose value added cannot be easily assessed.

5.21 These problems are undoubtedly formidable, and they embrace many others of detailed day to day administration which cannot be foreseen and yet which are crucial in determining the social acceptability of any form of taxation. Industrial opinion also suggests that there are apprehensions about the administrative burdens on industry, and it is widely felt that the introduction of a VAT would only be justified if there were offsetting simplifications made elsewhere in the fiscal system.

5.22 The practicability of a VAT in the UK must therefore very largely depend on the extent to which these very real administrative difficulties could be reduced or overcome, or offset by simplifications elsewhere. In considering how this might be done it is relevant that if we were to become members of the EEC, and were required to adopt the present EEC system, the difficulties would *have* to be overcome. Moreover, not all the problems which have been noted above are exclusive to a VAT. Some of them exist in varying degrees with our present taxes (for example, anomalies and borderline cases are not unknown with purchase tax and SET), and some would arise with any new tax, especially one which involved substantially broadening the base of indirect taxation to include services and a wide range of presently untaxed goods.

5.23 The introduction of a VAT would inevitably take time, probably at least two or three years from the time that the primary decisions were taken and depending on the other tax changes and administrative considerations involved. Experience in Europe shows that the ground needs to be carefully prepared, even when starting from the basis of an existing comprehensive turnover tax; but it is important that the problems of the transition should be carefully distinguished from those of a continuing nature. The former would be affected by the way in which the introduction of the tax was phased. The severity of the administrative problems would also depend on the range of rates and exemptions, the frequency of inspections, the complexity of the documentation, and the extent to which the system could be automated and computerised. Until these conditions are determined any estimate of the scale of the administrative problems must remain speculative, but it is worth recording that the Danes have, by the adoption of a single rate of tax, an extremely simple documentation procedure, and the comprehensive use of computers and the Post Office Giro system, presented themselves with few administrative difficulties. Difficulties would also be likely to be reduced if the tax were to be applied after an adequate period for adjustment and preparation.

5.24 Comparison with the experience of other countries may, however, be misleading where the scale of their economies and their past fiscal history may be very different from our own. Thus in the case of Denmark the wholesale stage tax which preceded the VAT was very much more broadly based than our purchase tax, so that both conceptually and in relation to the increase in the number of taxpayers the transition from the one system to the other was less abrupt than it would be in the UK. Any comparisons on a descriptive basis between one country and another can only provide pointers to the kinds of difficulty which have arisen and the methods which have been adopted to overcome them in those countries. Nevertheless, it is always possible to draw conclusions and learn lessons from these experiences which may be capable of adaptation to the circumstances of the UK economy.

5.25 Moreover, it is insufficient to assess the economic significance of these issues in qualitative terms alone. Insofar as all taxation involves administrative costs and personnel the question is whether the additional costs of a VAT would be worth incurring. Some rough estimate of these administrative costs can be made. Very broadly, the present average costs of tax collection in the UK work out at a little over 1 per cent of the total revenue collected (some taxes of course are cheaper than others). It is not known precisely what the equivalent rate is in other countries, but it has been suggested that in Europe it is around 2–3 per cent. Whether this is due to VAT or to other administrative considerations in these countries is impossible to say.

5.26 One estimate which has been made of the total staffing requirements of a VAT has put the figure at about 8,000*. On the basis of the 1967 average annual costs of HM Customs and Excise staff of about £1,850 per head, this would imply a total of some £16 million. The figure is now likely to be somewhat higher because of salary revisions, but so of course would be

* The exact number of full-time staff required to administer a VAT will, of course, depend upon the precise form and coverage of the tax and what other taxes are eliminated. (See eg Hansard, February 2 1971, Col. 321.)

the tax yield. Thus the VAT would have to raise on 1967 figures about £1,600 million (gross) to maintain the existing cost/yield ratio, which is within the range which would be likely with the kind of rates and exemptions which were discussed in the previous section. If economies of scale, which a comprehensive tax might make possible, could be secured the costs per head might be reduced well below the £1,850 figure. However, the major staff requirements would be likely to arise from the verification and control procedures rather than from the actual tax collection, which is where the major economies of scale would be most likely to arise.

5.27 The introduction of such a major tax change as a VAT could, however, call for a more substantial alteration in administrative practices than simply feeding it in to one of the already heavily burdened revenue departments, who cannot be expected to welcome the prospect of having their already formidable burdens increased. It could well be that the functions of the two existing revenue departments would need to be reappraised in the light of the new situation to ensure that the particular expertise and facilities of each were used in an optimal way. Also, instead of relying on the total coverage of traders by regular and frequent inspections, as is the case with purchase tax, this could be replaced or supplemented by spot checks and by maintaining appropriately severe penalties for evasion. It would, however, be necessary to consider carefully whether any lowering of the standards of revenue collection, to which we have become accustomed, would be acceptable, and it is the view of the revenue departments that such a decline would be inevitable. It is outside the scope of this Report to consider these operational problems in detail, but it is necessary to put the view that the reshaping of the tax structure might need to be accompanied by changes in departmental responsibilities if the benefits were to be maximised and the difficulties reduced.

5.28 From industry's point of view, once questions of taxable valuation and liability had been determined, the main problems would depend on how burdensome was the continuing task of aggregating sales and purchases in the form required for the VAT, and of working out the tax liabilities and credits resulting therefrom. The procedures themselves would be largely of a routine nature, but they would present a problem for smaller firms for whom specially simplified arrangements might have to be devised, and firms in general would almost certainly require additional clerical staff. At the same time, the introduction of a VAT could act as a stimulus to the mechanisation and improvement of accounting procedures in those small business enterprises where such improvements in technique would be highly productive.

5.29 Another aspect of VAT which it may be appropriate to consider, and which springs directly from the way in which an invoice-based VAT is administered and collected, relates to the provision and availability of economic information.

5.30 The British economy has suffered from a lack of comprehensive and up to date information on production and distribution, and the advantages which a monthly tax would provide for the purposes of economic forecasting and planning arises from the availability of computers to collate rapidly invoice information received from individual enterprises. The French administration is able to get a good indication of economic movements very quickly from the analysis of the returns of a selected sample of 2,000 large enterprises. An analysis of all returns would provide a virtually complete transactions matrix by region as well as by industry and could replace much of the statistical material now collected on a less comprehensive and less reliable basis.

VAT as an alternative to corporate taxes

5.31 The preceding sections of this chapter have shown that a VAT would be capable of raising large sums in revenue, and that it would also require considerable administrative changes to be made. Both of these considerations point to the need for the simultaneous abolition or modification of some taxes which now exist. Much of the earlier discussion of VAT, including that of the Richardson Committee, has examined the implications of a switch from the taxation of corporate profits towards the VAT, and in particular it has been argued that in theory an equal yield switch* of this kind would produce the following benefits:

a for investment
b for efficiency (to the extent that efficiency can be measured by profitability)
c for the balance of payments.

In the following paragraphs the theoretical principles underlying these propositions are examined in turn.

Investment effects

5.32 So far as investment is concerned, the argument that a VAT would tend to discriminate in favour of capital-intensive firms is, strictly, independent of a reduction in corporation tax. What the effect *does* depend upon is the new relationship, after the introduction of a VAT, between the price level of capital goods (including VAT) and the level of money wages. If, for example, the cost of all goods and services, including capital goods, rose by the full amount of VAT *and there was no consequent increase in money wages* then the rate of profit of both the more and less mechanised firms would be equally affected. If on the other hand wages were to rise in consequence of the VAT, then the situation is different: each firm experiences an increase in the price of its capital inputs and is compensated for this through the VAT credit mechanism for tax-invoiced purchases. However, each firm *further* experiences an indirect effect of VAT upon its money wage bill; and this is not compensated for. The impact of this cost increase will be greater for the firm with the higher ratio of direct labour to output. The case is illustrated and further argued in Annex 1, Example 3.

* *ie in which the revenue lost by the corporation tax was exactly replaced by a value added tax at the appropriate rate.*

5.33 A different case arises if the introduction of a VAT is accompanied, and compensated for, by a reduction in corporation tax. If the effect of this is the total or partial absorption of the VAT by capital goods producers, then the higher VAT base (essentially the sum of wages and profits) of the labour-intensive firm compared with the capital-intensive one is not fully offset by the increase in the cost of capital equipment purchases facing the capital-intensive firm. The latter thus gains an advantage in profit, both before and after corporation tax, over its less mechanised competitor. If, further, it is *adding* to its capital stock, and if the tax switch has reduced to any extent the VAT-*exclusive* cost of plant and equipment, then it enjoys a further advantage (assuming a buffer rule is not applied) from the immediate granting of a VAT credit on these purchases which exceeds the net increase in their tax-inclusive cost.

5.34 These are all effects which, if they occurred, would tend to improve the profitability of the more mechanised firms relative to the less mechanised. If as a result there was a redistribution of resources between these firms, this would tend to increase the capital-intensiveness of production generally. There could also be a new incentive to invest for each firm, with the less mechanised firms seeking to enjoy the tax advantages of the more mechanised. In every industry where any freedom of choice in the degree of mechanisation exists, this opportunity and incentive for greater mechanisation could be found.

5.35 Returning to the original argument in paragraph 5.31, where a VAT is introduced without a compensating reduction in corporation tax, it has to be emphasised that if the effect of the introduction of a VAT were to cause the prices of all capital goods to rise by the full amount of the VAT and yet to leave the cost of labour unchanged, then the incentive to mechanisation would disappear. Both more and less mechanised firms would be paying the same (tax-exclusive) price for their capital inputs as before and the same price for their labour inputs. Provided the tax-exclusive price of capital goods falls (eg because there is some saving of corporation tax to be taken into account) there will be an incentive to increase capital-intensiveness. Alternatively or additionally, if the effect of VAT on the price level of consumer goods tends to raise unit labour costs proportionately more than it *further* raises the costs of capital goods, an incentive to mechanisation exists. It is clear that in this case account must be taken of secondary increases in wage costs. The importance of these effects cannot be estimated without empirical evidence.

Efficiency effects

5.36 For efficiency (as measured by profitability) the argument is along the following lines: the more profitable firms gain back in absolute terms more in taxable profits than do the less profitable, and have both the opportunity and the incentive to become more profitable still. It should be borne in mind, however, that if two firms, one more profitable than the other, have the same ratios of labour to capital costs then their relative profits and profitability, one to the other, will remain unchanged after the tax switch. But the reduction in corporation tax will, of course, change their total post-tax profits by different absolute amounts. The efficiency argument is set out and illustrated in Example 1 of Annex 1 to this chapter.

Balance of payments effects

5.37 For exports, the argument is again similar in principle. If there is a switch from taxes that are not rebated on exports (eg the corporation tax) to taxes that are, this strengthens the financial position of the exporter relatively to the non-exporter and gives him the opportunity and incentive to export more, while the non-exporter has a greater incentive to export for the first time. This argument is set out and illustrated in Example 2 of the Annex.

5.38 However, the possibility of cost increases brought about by the VAT has to be allowed for. If corporation tax is not reflected at all in prices, and VAT is passed on in full, then there is no immediate change in the relative profitability of home and export markets. The exporter recovers in full the tax levied on his inputs but does not enjoy, as does the producer for the home market, the higher, tax-inclusive, selling price. If VAT is only partly passed on, or the cut in corporation tax is partly reflected in prices, so that tax-exclusive prices on the home market fall a little, there remains the danger that because of the inevitable increase in the tax-inclusive prices of final goods on the home market, wages may rise and hence prices again, in an inflationary spiral, so that ultimately domestic costs have risen by as much as or more than the VAT. Apart from this possibility, and other things being equal, exporting becomes relatively more profitable. Even if little of corporation tax and all of value added tax are passed on in prices there is still an increase in the relative profitability of exporting. The possible relevance of this theoretical argument is attested to by the attention being paid in the USA to the effect on its competitive position of the increasing diffusion of value added tax through Europe.

5.39 There are further considerations for the balance of payments as a whole which would arise if there were to be a tax switch involving the introduction of VAT. On the positive side, a difference is introduced between imported final consumer goods and home-produced import substitutes. Both pay VAT on the whole of their value. However, while nothing, presumably, happens to the rate of profits tax paid by the producers of imports, the domestic producers enjoy a lower rate of tax on their profits than otherwise. Their ability to compete effectively with imports, whether by price or non-price competition, is therefore increased. On the negative side, a reduction in corporation tax will damage the balance on invisible account by reducing the taxation of interest, profits and dividends accruing to foreigners. On the other hand, there might be some effect on the long term capital account arising from the reduced corporation tax rate which would rule. The likely final net effect upon the balance of payments is difficult to estimate and would have to be the subject of further and more detailed study.

5.40 In 1964 the Richardson Committee examined these theoretical arguments, but rejected them. On the balance of payments proposition they agreed that a substitution of v a t for corporate taxation could encourage exports and import substitution *so long as the general price level did not rise by as much as the full amount of the VAT*. If it did then any advantages would be lost. On general grounds, supported by the views of the businessmen from whom the Committee took evidence, they concluded that, taking into account secondary effects on prices through wages, the substitution 'would be more likely to harm than to benefit the balance of payments'. That is to say the general price level *would* be likely to rise by more than the amount of the v a t. So far as the efficiency arguments are concerned, the Richardson Committee concluded that these could be given little support. Businessmen, they argued, were mostly concerned with the pre-tax profits position and there was little sign that they would be affected in their investment decisions by cuts in corporate taxation. Even those who did take account of the post-tax profits situation were unlikely to be influenced in their investment decisions.

5.41 It seems now, however, that there are some grounds for reconsidering these questions. After looking at the theoretical arguments again, and taking views from industry through the e d cs, it seems that if a *substantial* cut in corporation tax were practicable, and if it were replaced by an equal yielding value added tax, then it is on balance more likely than the Richardson Committee concluded that some benefits to the balance of payments and efficiency could arise. The reasons why it is felt that the conclusions of the Richardson Committee may be modified on this issue are:

a The view, endorsed by some (though not all) of the e d cs that a cut in corporate taxes on businesses would lead to lower prices in the longer term, and, if the cut were great enough, possibly in the short term also.

b The intensification of the competitive climate resulting from trade liberalisation and the abolition of resale price maintenance will exert pressures against excessive price increases, and this has received some support from the post-devaluation experience.

c The growing sophistication of business accounting procedures is resulting in closer attention being paid to post-tax profitability, and the change from profits tax and income tax to corporation tax has also contributed in this direction.

5.42 The whole basis of this argument depends crucially on what happens to the general level of costs and prices; if they rise by the whole amount of the v a t then almost all the advantages are lost. Moreover, if the v a t were to be levied at a rate greater than that required to produce an equal yield to that lost by a cut in corporation tax, the likelihood is that prices *would* rise by more than the saving in corporation tax thus offsetting any competitive or cost advantage. Also the improvement in the competitive climate noted above is by no means uniform, and the cumulative effect of markups based on post-tax prices could lead to higher prices. Finally, it is likely that the amount of tax locked up in stocks, work in progress, and so on, at any one time could be very substantial.

5.43 Whatever the balance of this debate, in practical terms it seems likely that only a very small cut in corporation tax would be possible in the immediate future. First, this is because the tax has only recently been introduced and a major cut would alter its character. Secondly, a substantial reduction would involve a greater switch from the direct taxation of corporate profits to the indirect taxation of goods and services than would be regarded as socially tolerable unless it were accompanied by compensatory measures. Thirdly, it has been argued, existing taxes on corporate profits in the UK are not high by international standards, and in particular as compared with the EEC (although a crude comparison of corporation tax rates leaves out of account differences in the treatment of dividends).

5.44 A small cut in corporation tax replaced by an equal yielding value added tax at a low rate (say a $1\frac{1}{4}$ per cent VAT for 5 per cent corporation tax) would not yield the economic benefits suggested in paragraphs 5.31–5.39 above. The tax switch would have to be big enough to make a perceptible difference to a firm's cost position, and to make it worth while to try to increase its market share. A small cut could well be seen by businessmen as only temporary, and would therefore not influence their industrial policies. Since, for all the administrative reasons given in the previous section, it would not be worth introducing a VAT at a purely nominal rate, a rate higher than that required to replace the lost corporation tax revenue would be likely to raise prices by more than any cuts which might be made following the reduction in corporation tax, and therefore the balance of payments benefits resulting from the switch would be lost.

5.45 It should also be noted that a cut in corporation tax would not benefit the unincorporated sector of business, which includes a great many enterprises of all sizes, for example, in agriculture and the service trades as well as in parts of manufacturing industry. Neither would a cut in corporation tax benefit the nationalised industries, supplying coal, electricity, gas and steel, nor British Railways, the Post Office, nor the oil industry, because for various reasons which were described in the Report of the Richardson Committee, these industries pay little or no corporation tax. The problem of giving equivalent relief to these groups would be extremely difficult.

5.46 Therefore, unless or until a substantial cut in corporation tax (either by itself or in combination with other tax changes) was considered desirable, the case for considering the introduction of a VAT in the immediate future must rest primarily on whether it provides a viable basis for *other* adjustments in taxation and for extending the tax coverage to goods and services not at present included.

5.47 There is, however, one further consideration: while the possibility of substituting a VAT for a substantial cut in corporation tax may be so remote as to be unrealistic, it would perhaps not be so unreasonable to think of a VAT as a substitute for a substantial *increase* in corporation tax. If there were to be pressure for higher revenue the possibility of a further increase should certainly not be ruled out. In this case the theoretical implications of the differences in the economic impact of the two taxes would be highly relevant.

VAT and indirect taxation

5.48 Although it was argued in the previous section that the immediate and practical possibility of a major switch from corporation tax to a VAT was remote, this is by no means the only reason for examining the implications of a VAT in relation to indirect taxation. Indeed, while the theoretical arguments which have been rehearsed above are of interest in the continuing debate on the influence of taxation on business behaviour, the most immediate concern attaches to the possibility of using the VAT as a basis for the general taxation of goods and services because it may be a better instrument for so doing than those we have now.

5.49 It was seen in Chapter 3 that (even after allowing for the treatment of local rates) the present tax system in the UK is already quite heavily weighted towards indirect taxation, but that it falls on a relatively narrow range of consumers' expenditure. While this is a situation to which we in Britain have grown accustomed it is not one which is founded on any of the eternal verities, and it does undoubtedly have a number of serious disadvantages especially where the levels of taxation are as high as they are today. These disadvantages are not confined to the effect on consumers, but also affect the revenue and the management of the economy.

5.50 The following arguments have been advanced for enlarging the share and broadening the base of indirect taxation:
a That there is a case for shifting the balance of taxation from earned incomes to consumption as an incentive to work, saving, and the taking of risks.
b That the UK is approaching the limit of taxable capacity on many items of goods, especially tobacco and alcohol, which provide a large part of tax revenue; and of acceptability in certain areas of direct taxation on earned incomes, especially where there is a particularly rapid progression at certain points in the income scale.
c Since indirect taxation is concentrated on a narrow range of goods the use of these taxes as general regulators of the economy may distort demand to the detriment of particular industries, especially those producing durable consumer goods.
d The use of narrowly based taxes as a general regulator of demand is not wholly effective since it is likely to lead to the diversion of expenditure as well as to its reduction. This implies that when such taxes are increased, their influence on aggregate demand will be proportionately less than their

effect on the cost of living; to this extent they will be less deflationary than a broader based indirect tax increase.

e The broader the tax base, the lower can be the rate of tax required to raise any given amount of revenue, and this has presentational advantages.

f It can be argued that, except to achieve specified social and economic objectives, expenditure should be taxed in close proportion to the price of goods and services, and therefore the high tax rates required by a narrow tax base are undesirable.

5.51 It can, on the other hand, be argued that apart from the alternative possibility of broadening the total base of taxation by the extension of taxes on wealth and property, there is a case for retaining a substantial measure of selectivity and flexibility within even a more broadly based system of indirect taxation:

a The introduction of a broader and less differentiated system of indirect taxation might be expected to result in an initial rise in prices, which would have adverse effects on people on low incomes and could lead to widespread demands for compensatory increases in wages and social benefits. In general, indirect taxation *can* be applied in such a way as to promote a more equitable distribution of income, by taxing certain categories of consumption more heavily than others. The use of a selective expenditure tax would also be a means of reducing the burden of economic regulation on low-income groups, where it inevitably falls disproportionately heavily. These questions are examined in paragraphs 5.53–5.56, where the redistributive effects of purchase tax are compared with those of two possible versions of a VAT.

b One method of achieving economic objectives (such as regional redevelopment and the encouragement of exports and import substitution), based on agreed priorities, lies in the differential tax treatment of different economic sectors, whether industrial or geographical.

c The selective taxation of industries which impose heavy costs on the community is one possible means of equating private and social costs.

d There is a case for using indirect taxation to influence consumption patterns according to agreed social preferences.

5.52 Perhaps the most fundamental of these considerations is the effect which a broadening of the indirect tax base would have on income distribution. A broadening of the indirect tax base, whether by a VAT or any other method, would initially alter the relative prices to which people have become accustomed, and by bringing goods previously exempted within the scope of taxation could place new burdens on the lower income groups who would certainly demand compensation through direct increases in their incomes, through adjustments in other taxation (eg on earned incomes at the lower levels), or through improvements in benefits (such as old age pensions and family allowances).

5.53 It is extremely difficult to measure how great the effects of tax changes might be, because family sizes, incomes and expenditure patterns vary so widely. Nevertheless there is a conventional statistical device which may be employed for this purpose, namely the Gini coefficient of income inequality, which can provide an indication on a standardised, if crude, basis of the effects of changes in taxation and benefits on the distribution of real incomes.

5.54 Using this method a comparison was made by the Central Statistical Office, based on 1966 Family Expenditure data relating to incomes and family size, between the effect of purchase tax at 1968/69 rates on the one hand, and, on the other, the two illustrative VAT schemes described in paragraphs 5.9–5.13. (The indirect impact of VAT on exempt products—including foodstuffs—was estimated from input-output tables and included in the VAT effective yields. The estimated rates were 3 per cent on foodstuffs under Scheme A, where the assumed VAT rate is 10 per cent on all remaining items of consumer expenditure; and 4 per cent on the exempt items (foodstuffs, fuel and light, books, newspaper and magazines) under Scheme B.)

5.55 Gini coefficients of income inequality in percentage terms were estimated for net household income after direct benefits and personal income tax and for net household income less purchase tax on the one hand, and less VAT (A) and VAT (B) on the other. These coefficients can theoretically vary between 0 (which would represent a perfectly equal distribution of incomes) and 100 (representing a situation in which the whole of income accrued to one household). Coefficients were calculated separately for single person households and households with no children, 1 child, 2 children, 3 children and 4 children. Weighted average coefficients for all 6 types were also calculated.

5.56 For every £100 of tax paid per household, the alternative methods of raising it made insignificant differences to the Gini measure of income inequality. Whereas the effect of *direct benefits*, for example is to reduce the coefficient (ie to reduce inequalities) by 6·3 per cent by comparison with original income, the effect of purchase tax at 1968/69 rates applied to 1966 family expenditure is to *increase inequality* by 0·13 per cent overall per £100 per household of tax. That is to say purchase tax is very slightly regressive. The effect of the substitution of VAT (Scheme B) for purchase tax is to *increase inequality* by 0·21 per cent, ie by 0·08 per cent more than purchase tax, or a difference equal to a little over 1 per cent of the difference made by the payment of direct benefits. The effect of Scheme A (the flat 10 per cent tax, excluding foodstuffs) is to increase income inequality, per £100 per household of tax, by rather more, though still not very significantly, ie by one half of 1 per cent. Differences of the same general order of size show up for the six different categories of household with small individual variations. The largest increase in inequality as a result of substituting Scheme B for purchase tax, per £100 of tax, is 0·39 per cent for single adult households which would include widows and pensioners. At the other extreme, Scheme B *reduces* inequality, by comparison with purchase tax, per £100 of tax per household, by 0·09 per cent for households with 2 adults and 2 children. It therefore seems that there is little substance in the fear that the substitution of a VAT, certainly if applied at two rates and with food and certain other exemptions, would be so inequitable as to be incapable of correction by way of quite small adjustments in direct benefits such as pensions or family allowances.

5.57 There is the possibility, however, that the *introduction* of a new broadly based tax, as distinct from its continuing application could have a once and for all adverse effect on prices and income distribution resulting from the 'ratchet' phenomenon in which prices are more likely to be increased by the application of a new tax then reduced by the removal of an old one.

5.58 Any change in indirect taxation produces effects on relative prices and real incomes. A decision to broaden the tax base, by bringing hitherto untaxed or lowly taxed goods and services into the net, will have effects similar to those just discussed: they are not the exclusive consequence of a VAT. However, the question remains, even if it is agreed that there should be additional emphasis on the indirect taxation of consumers' expenditure and that this should be accomplished by extending the coverage of indirect taxation, is a VAT the best method to adopt?

VAT or an extended purchase tax?

5.59 It has been argued that, whatever might be achieved in the way of encouragement to exporting, import substitution, capital investment and increasing industrial efficiency by way of a VAT, it could as well be achieved by an extension of single stage taxation of consumer expenditure: for example, by widening the coverage of purchase tax. What then are the merits and demerits of VAT as compared with some elaboration of the existing single stage taxation of domestic consumer expenditure?

5.60 One possibility, which regards purchase tax as itself a version of a VAT, (with suspension of tax at earlier stages) and grafting onto it a retail stage VAT, is discussed in Annex 2 to this chapter. It is not clear, however, whether it would fall within the rules laid down in the EEC directives on VAT, and it also has practical drawbacks as the Annex shows. The strict alternative to a VAT would be a more comprehensive and uniform purchase tax, supplemented by a separate system for taxing retail distribution and services, such as the SET.

5.61 One first difference lies in the width of coverage of the two systems. Although in principle it need not be so, in practice it is likely that the coverage of a VAT would be wider than that of an extended purchase tax. A VAT is essentially a general comprehensive tax with specific exemptions; the purchase tax is, by contrast, particular, with specific inclusions, in order to restrict taxation, as far as possible, to goods which are purchased largely by final consumers. The VAT, because of the operation of tax credits for business purchases, does not need to make this distinction and thus, in this respect, avoids difficulties and anomalies arising from difficulties of definition. Clearly therefore in the case of a VAT the fewer the exemptions or other forms of differential treatment the simpler the tax, whereas with purchase tax simplicity and the avoidance of anomalies is derived from *limiting* its coverage. Even when exemption from VAT is allowed, the goods involved are not entirely free of the tax, since their prices will incorporate the tax which cannot be recovered on value added on the products of other industries providing taxed inputs.

5.62 It is the view of HM Customs and Excise that it would be technically possible to extend the existing system of tax free purchases by registered traders and so to achieve much the same position in regard to the taxation of goods under the purchase tax as under a VAT while still avoiding the worst complexities of multi-stage taxation. If this is the case, then, given the need to do everything possible to assist the balance of payments, it would seem desirable to extend it if it is, at the same time as being 'technically' possible, economically worthwhile and internationally acceptable.

5.63 It is also probable that the extension of purchase tax would tend to involve a less uniform tax rate structure than would be practicable with a VAT, given the built in disadvantages of a multiplicity of rates of VAT, and in particular the desirability of limiting the area in which net tax refunds are regularly paid. (It is noteworthy in this connection that in the 1968 Budget the number of purchase tax rates was increased from three to four.) This raises the question of the merits of alternative tax systems that are more and less selective in their impact on different consumer goods services. On the one hand the diversity of social and economic objectives and criteria which exists would call for very considerable variations in tax rates to achieve them. On the other hand administrative considerations require that the number of variations should be reduced as much as possible. Any practical scheme of taxation represents a compromise which wholly satisfies neither criterion.

5.64 The discussion of the effects of a VAT on income distribution in paragraphs 5.52–5.56 has indicated that greater selectivity, such as is possible with purchase tax, can be used to minimise any adverse effects in this direction, although the size of this problem appeared to be small.

5.65 Greater selectivity also makes it possible to discriminate between industries and regions on the basis of their likely contributions to the balance of payments, the rate of economic growth or the reduction of regional unemployment. On the other hand in practice, selectivity in indirect taxation is usually designed to prevent these taxes from having too regressive an effect, or to discriminate between goods according to social judgements about their relative necessity. It is unlikely that the same pattern of selectivity would result from these criteria as would be indicated by the requirements of growth, balance of payments or efficiency. Furthermore, while not necessarily selective as between different consumer goods and services, VAT, by effectively taxing only final domestic consumption, does avoid taxing exports, and does not tax both capital investment and the consumer goods and services to which the investment contributes. Regional selectivity, outside the field of income taxation and investment grants, is currently achieved by way of the Regional Employment Premium (REP). There does not appear to be any reason why the REP should not survive whatever method of taxing goods and services generally were adopted.

5.66 Indirect taxes are employed, not simply as a means of raising revenue, but also and increasingly as an economic regulator. The narrower the base of indirect taxes and the more discriminatory the rates of tax on particular goods, the more likely it is that any increase in these taxes will result not in a lowering of consumption expenditure but in its diversion towards untaxed or lower taxed goods or services. This implies that, in order to achieve a given reduction in demand, prices must rise by more the narrower is the range of goods to which the regulator applies. In the case of a fully comprehensive indirect tax, there is nothing that can be substituted for consumption except saving. The extent to which real consumption will decline depends, in either case, upon the extent to which consumers seek to and are able to maintain the rate of growth of real consumption they desire, and this in turn depends upon a number of factors including existing consumer wealth, the flow of personal saving that can be drawn upon and the availability of consumer credit. But these factors are not affected by the choice of tax system.

5.67 It may be added that where a tax regulator depends heavily upon changes in the tax on beer and cigarettes, its incidence upon people with low incomes may be as heavy as, or heavier than, a regulator applied to a more comprehensive range of goods and services.

5.68 The advantage of the purchase tax compared with the VAT as a regulator is its flexibility. Regulatory changes in a VAT, while involving probably rather smaller changes in tax rates, would involve bigger changes for industry and the Government because of the larger number of taxpayers.

5.69 Since tax is collected at each stage of production under a VAT, and only at the wholesale stage under purchase tax, an increase in the rate of VAT would have an impact upon producers at early stages of production, which a 'regulatory' increase in the purchase tax does not have. Whether such producers as a whole would have liquidity problems will depend upon the exact timing and volume of their sales at the new tax rate. What is clear, however, is that a regulatory increase in VAT would result in a swifter benefit to the exporter (who recovers the whole of the VAT passed on to him without any offsetting tax liability) where he is competing with producers for the domestic market for a limited supply of *intermediate* goods.

5.70 It is a criticism of purchase tax that, although it is not directly levied on producer goods, there is some spill over into industrial costs and hence into the price of exports and capital goods. Under a VAT, the relief of exports from all the taxation levied upon inputs into those exports is automatic, except where some particular item of expenditure (like business purchases of cars under the French VAT régime) is expressly disallowed. Under a purchase tax régime, unregistered businesses (which could include exporters) do not enjoy tax relief in respect of purchases of goods which have passed through the taxed stage. Registered businesses, on the other hand, are entitled to relief in respect of taxable materials used in manufacture, but not in respect of taxable items such as stationery nor motor cars used in the business. The effect of this spill over is not *at present* particularly important: it was estimated in 1969 that about 13 per cent of purchase tax revenue accrued from the sale of goods to businesses (much of it arising from the sale of cars) and of this, perhaps one-fifth (£20 million) probably entered into export costs. The introduction of a more wide-ranging, comprehensive purchase tax would, however, significantly increase the element of unrebated taxation entering into exports (But see paragraph 5.62.)

5.71 Under the present tax arrangements a much more important cause of spill-over of taxation into industrial costs, and hence into exports, is the hydrocarbon oil duties. It was largely to neutralise this effect that the export rebate, equivalent to about 2 per cent of export turnover, was introduced and maintained up to the time of devaluation in 1967. In the absence now of this rebate, any large switch of emphasis from hydrocarbon oil duties towards a VAT would significantly relieve industrial costs and exports from indirect taxation.

5.72 There is a parallel difference between the incidence of purchase tax and VAT upon capital goods. Both have the same intention, namely to tax only final consumer goods. The VAT system achieves this by allowing credits to purchasers for all taxes levied on business purchases, including retail purchases, and purchases of plant and equipment. By this means, all contributions to final domestic consumption (including the contribution of capital equipment in the current period, ie depreciation) are taxed once and once only. In the absence of a 'buffer rule', no net VAT is levied on net capital formation; a tax credit is received by the purchaser, with no offsetting VAT liability. With a purchase tax (particularly if its scope was extended, and even although most identifiable capital goods and equipment would be excluded), because there is no automatic rebating of tax paid on inputs, there is the risk that, unless special counter measures were taken, a part of indirect taxes could fall on net capital formation, to the extent that producers of plant and equipment buy goods from unregistered businesses.

5.73 The difference between the two systems, so far as their impact on capital investment is concerned, lies solely in this element of double taxation, that arises (at present to a rather small extent) under a purchase tax system (unless modified as has been suggested in paragraph 5.62). It is quite incorrect to suppose that VAT, of itself, 'subsidises' investment (any more than it 'subsidises' exports), or differs from purchase tax in its treatment of investment goods in any other respect than that described here. (The 'mechanisation effect' referred to in paragraph 5.31 is a possible consequence of any 'pure' consumption tax, added to an existing tax structure, and arises if the effect of the tax is to increase the ratio of the price of labour to the *tax-exclusive* price of capital).

5.74 The difference between VAT and other forms of indirect taxation may be summed up as follows. In its purest form, where there are no exempt sectors and no buffer rule operates, VAT in no way enters into industrial costs: it is passed on, and fully recovered, by all businesses, up to the point of transfer to the eventual final consumer in the domestic economy; by contrast, purchase tax (at present to a small extent), excise duties like the fuel taxes, and the SET (both even now, to a significant extent) do enter costs in an irrecoverable way, including the costs of exports and of plant and equipment. The importance of this arises not simply in relation to present circumstances, but in the way in which the indirect tax system develops in the future.

5.75 Because of the operation of a fractional payments system in which tax credits are dependent upon the production of purchase invoices, the VAT system is to a certain extent self-enforcing (see Chapter 2, paragraph 2.28), and only a fraction of the yield is at risk at any one point in the chain of production and distribution. With any single-stage alternative, like purchase tax, the whole of the yield is at risk at the taxable stage, and not just the tax on the value added by the seller at that stage. This presents no serious enforcement problems under the present purchase tax régime, where only about 65,000 registered traders are selling to unregistered purchasers. But greater difficulties of enforcing purchase tax might arise if its scope was widely extended, with a corresponding increase in the number of registered traders from whom the whole of the tax would be collected. These considerations should be set against the difficulties of enforcement which would arise with the much larger number of traders who would be involved in a VAT.

5.76 One of the most important characteristics of a VAT is its universality, and for this reason it presents no special problems in relation to the taxation of services and value added in retailing, save those of control, particularly of small businesses. The extension of a purchase tax system would still leave out retail gross margins, which are included in the coverage of a comprehensive VAT, and substantial modification of the existing purchase tax system would be necessary to deal with consumer services. It may be assumed that these areas would continue to be taxed by way of SET.

The estimated net yield of SET in 1969 was a little over £800 million. This was equivalent to a little over 3 per cent of consumer's expenditure, and was therefore, from the point of view of yield, an alternative to about an additional 3 per cent VAT. However, the incidence of SET on various goods and services, dependent as it is upon the ratios of full time employment to output, varies quite widely. Apart from its non-neutrality between different goods and services, and between different companies, with and without establishments devoted mainly to manufacturing, the SET, in practice, creates a problem of overspill, without rebate, into manufacturing costs, and hence into the costs of goods for export and of plant and equipment for research and development. The SET is in many ways a convenient tax, but it cannot be designed so as to distinguish between service *inputs* into other services and manufacturing (including exports), and *pure consumer services*, so as to tax the latter but not the former. Such distinction is automatic under the VAT invoice system. The SET, on the other hand, retains the advantages of selectivity: it is possible to alter the rate of tax on employment in the service sector, without at the same time changing the rate of tax in manufacturing. (Regional selectivity, as was noted in paragraph 5.65 does not essentially depend upon the survival of a SET.) There are both advantages and disadvantages of a separate services tax based on full time employment levels, rather than upon payroll or turnover. These questions go beyond the scope of this report.

5.77　There are also differences between VAT and purchase tax in the timing of Exchequer receipts. A single-stage and a fractional payments tax differ in the speed with which revenue from the tax builds up, when either the level of activity or the rate of tax increases. If, for example, VAT rates are raised, tax yields immediately increase by the increment of tax applied to the whole of final consumer goods sales in that period (as with a change in purchase tax) but, in addition, by the tax rate increment, applied to value added at all stages of production in that period. The restrictive effect on consumer demand is thus reinforced without delay, by a mopping-up of business liquidity from all outlays other than on exports or net capital formation. The effect upon the demand for real resources is likely to be felt swiftly, right down the production chain.

5.78　There remains one further possible difference between fractional payments system and a single-stage tax such as the purchase tax. If, at some future time, a decision was taken to change the distribution of taxation between direct taxes, like corporation tax and income tax, and indirect taxes, the effect on the general level of prices of such a shift of emphasis would be likely to be more inflationary if indirect taxation depended upon the purchase tax than if it depended upon a VAT. This is because, under a single-stage purchase tax system, there is no correspondence between the savings of corporation tax on the one hand and the liability to indirect tax on the other. Purchase tax is collected at the wholesale stage, at which the saving of corporation tax would be negligible compared with the liability to purchase tax. Nor, given the well known downward rigidity of prices, will there be likely to be compensating reductions in prices at the earlier stages of production where all that has happened is a saving of corporation tax. On balance prices would be likely to rise by the whole of the increase in purchase tax in that case. Under a fractional payments tax system, like VAT, if, at some future time, the emphasis of taxation were changed, the saving of corporation tax would affect firms at every stage of production and would run in parallel with the new VAT liability at those same stages (although, of course, not necessarily with perfectly offsetting symmetry, especially having regard again to the 'ratchet' effect on prices). The opportunity, at each stage, for each taxpayer to set off the one tax against the other, could result in rather more stability of prices than when indirect taxation relied primarily upon a single-stage tax like purchase tax.

5.79   Finally, there remains the question of our possible future membership of the European Economic Community. Although the possibility must not be altogether ruled out that we might be able to negotiate with the six to retain our existing single-stage purchase tax (arguing for its similarity, as far as it goes, to a system of VAT with purchases 'under suspension of tax'*), there can be no doubt, particularly now that the Scandinavian countries have adopted VAT, that its introduction will probably be a condition of membership of the Community. In any event, the introduction of a VAT would put our system of taxation on all fours with one of our most important trading areas, so far as the treatment of imports and exports is concerned.

5.80   A number of the differences between a purchase tax system and a VAT discussed above, suggest that a VAT system has some advantages over a purchase tax system. There is no way of quantifying these, and in the last resort, as with any other tax question, a final decision must rest on individual judgment and political decision. One thing is clear; whatever weight may be attached to these, or any other arguments in favour of a VAT, on the other side of the balance must be placed the administrative costs associated with:
   a   A large increase in the number of separate tax-collection points
   b   The invoicing of tax on every sale between businesses
   c   The periodic calculation and reporting and payment of net VAT by businesses

*See Annex 2 to this chapter.

d The verification of the year's tax payments, possibly at the same time as corporation tax and company income tax.

Against these, can be set the saving of administrative costs associated with purchase tax and the SET, and any incidental advantages resulting from the increased flow of short term statistics of sales and purchases.

5.81 Most of the putative long run effects—on exports, import-substitution, mechanisation and efficiency—depend upon a redirection of taxation, under certain assumptions, towards indirect taxes and away from direct taxes; they do *not* depend on the direct tax being corporation tax and the indirect tax being a VAT. Some differences may be found between existing indirect taxes, in particular purchase tax and SET, and a VAT; and the most important of these are probably the differences in the breadth and uniformity of coverage likely in practice; the spill-over of other indirect taxes into net capital formation and exports; and the commitment of the rest of Europe to VAT. On the other side of the balance sheet the administrative problems represent the most weighty item.

5.82 If, as a matter of policy, it is felt that a wider coverage in indirect taxation is undesirable, then a VAT is inappropriate. But there is clearly a case for considering the validity of the argument that the higher is the ratio of those indirect taxes that do not fall, or can be rebated, on exports and net capital formation to all other taxes, including direct taxes and fuel duties which enter industrial costs without rebate, the better for the balance of payments and for growth in the capital stock.

Annex 1

**Illustrations of the possible
effects of tax changes
involving a VAT upon the
relative profitability of
'efficient' firms, exporters
and more highly
mechanised firms**

5.83 The three examples in this annex are numerical illustrations of the changes
in the distribution of total taxation between different kinds of firm that
might follow from changes in the tax system, especially changes involving
a reduction in corporation tax and the introduction of a VAT. Certain
assumptions are made, and it is assumed that, apart from these, other things
remain unchanged. In each example, two firms, A and B, are considered,
each with the same total sales, but differing from each other in one
important respect. In Example 1, A has higher labour productivity than B
(expressed in the form of lower unit wage costs), but is in all other respects
identical with it. In Example 2, A exports part of its output, and B does not;
the two firms are in all other respects identical. In Example 3, A is more
mechanised than B (ie, has a higher ratio of capital to labour), but is the
same in all other respects, including having the same initial net rate of
return on capital as does B.

5.84 In the first two examples, the position of the two firms is shown first where
corporation tax stands at 45 per cent and there is no VAT (column 1).
In columns 2 to 4, the position is shown after a reduction of corporation tax
to 40 per cent and the imposition of a VAT of approximately equal yield
at the rate of $2\frac{1}{2}$ per cent. The absolute and relative profitability of the two
firms is shown after the tax switch for three sample situations. In the first
of these (column 2), it is assumed that neither prices, inclusive of VAT,
nor money wages change. In the second (column 3), it is assumed that
the VAT is passed on in full by both the firms, but that money wages do
not change: hence the ratio of wages to net profits falls. In the third
situation (column 4), the assumption is that the VAT is passed on in full,
and it is further assumed that there is also an increase in money wages
sufficient to maintain the ratio of wages to net profits unchanged. In the
bottom row of each example, the effect of the tax change on the relative
profitability of the two firms after tax is shown.

5.85 In the third example, where the two firms differ in their degree of
mechanisation, the position is again shown first with corporation tax at
45 per cent and no VAT (column 1). In columns 2 to 4, sample results are
shown for the two firms when a 5 per cent VAT is introduced, *without* any
offsetting reduction in corporation tax. The example illustrates that this
possible differential effect, to the detriment of the less mechanised firm B,
does *not* depend upon the reduction of corporation tax. It is assumed that
all prices (including the prices of capital goods) rise by the full amount
of the VAT. The assumptions are that in column 2, there is no consequent
change in money wages; in column 3, wages increase by $2\frac{1}{2}$ per cent;
and in column 4, the increase in money wages matches the increase in the
cost of living resulting from the introduction of the uncompensated VAT
at 5 per cent. On the bottom row of example 3, the consequences for the
rate of return on capital after tax are shown for the two firms.

5.86 Throughout the three examples, the VAT payable by the firm is calculated on the 'tax-from-tax' or 'invoicing' basis: that is to say, it consists of the element of VAT in the value of home sales less the VAT element in the value of purchases. This can be read off in a straightforward way, except where it is assumed that the VAT is absorbed by the producer (column 2 in examples 1 and 2). In example 1, column 2, for example, the VAT payable by both A and B is approximately 2·5 on a tax-*exclusive* value of home sales of about 97·5 (assuming the VAT to be fully absorbed), *less* approximately 1·25 on a tax-*exclusive* cost of purchases of approximately 48·75 (if the VAT again is fully absorbed).

Example 1

5.87 In column 1 of example 1, A earns higher profits than B because of its lower labour requirements, and hence higher profits after corporation tax. In fact, A's profits are twice those of B. While the reduction of corporation tax to 40 per cent, in column 2, will not of itself change this profit ratio, the $2\frac{1}{2}$ per cent VAT, which is an equal burden on both firms, changes the ratio of the profits of the two firms, both before and after corporation tax, from 2 to 2·14. Thus, in the example, if no firm alters its final prices, including VAT, A's after-tax profits increase by 0·25 and B's decrease by the same amount. It would appear that, if A and B are in competition, A might with advantage absorb the VAT, making it difficult for B to maintain its profitability. If, however (column 3), all prices, including the price of the purchases made by the two firms, increase in proportion to the VAT, both firms maintain their absolute profits before tax at the original

Example 1   A has a lower ratio of wages to value added than B

	(1) 45% corporation tax; nil VAT		(2) no price change no wage change		(3) $2\frac{1}{2}$% price change no wage change		(4) $2\frac{1}{2}$% price change no change in wages/net profit ratio	
	A	B	A	B	A	B	A	B
Home sales	100	100	100	100	102·5	102·5	102·5	102·5
Wage bill	30	40	30	40	30	40	30·77	41·03
Purchases (including depreciation)	50	50	50	50	51·25	51·25	51·25	51·25
VAT payable	—	—	1·25	1·25	1·25	1·25	1·25	1·25
Base of corporation tax	20	10	18·75	8·75	20	10	19·23	8·97
Corporation tax	9	4·5	7·5	3·5	8	4	7·68	3·59
Profits after all taxes	11	5·5	11·25	5·25	12	6	11·55	5·38
Change in total tax paid	—	—	−0·25	+0·25	+0·25	+0·75	−0·07	+1·13
Wages/profits after tax	4·24		4·24		3·89		4·24	
Ratio of A's net profits to B's net profits	2·0		2·14		2·0		2·14	

level; and the ratio of their profits after tax remains at 2. Because wages are assumed not to have changed, the profits of both firms rise by the 5 per cent reduction in corporation tax (1·0 for A and 0·5 for B). The ratio of wages to net profits will have fallen, however, and it may be thought that the old volume of sales could not easily be made and that there would be a tendency for wages to rise to restore the original income distribution. In that event, the situation illustrated in column 4 might arise. Here, B suffers from the indirect effect of the VAT on its wage bill, which is higher than A's, wage rates having risen by about 2·5 per cent to restore the original distribution of income. Now both total profits and total wages are unchanged in real terms as a consequence of the equal yield tax switch; but A does better than B, just as it did in column 2, where total profits and wages were unchanged in both real terms and money terms.

Example 2

5.88 In column 1 of example 2, the profits of A and B are equal, both before and after 45 per cent corporation tax. In fact, the only difference between the two firms is that exports account for two-fifths of A's total sales revenue. Their wage bills and outside purchases are the same. VAT is levied on home sales only, less a credit for the VAT element in purchases whatever their destination. In column 2, a $2\frac{1}{2}$ per cent VAT replaces the yield of 5 per cent of corporation tax, and it is assumed that the VAT is everywhere

Example 2 A exports and B does not

	(1) 45% corporation tax; nil VAT		(2) no price change no wage change		(3) $2\frac{1}{2}$% price change no wage change		(4) $2\frac{1}{2}$% price change no change in wages/net profits ratio	
			40% corporation tax; $2\frac{1}{2}$% VAT					
	A	B	A	B	A	B	A	B
Export sales (value)	40*	0	40*	0	40*	0	40*	0
Home sales (value)	60	100	60	100	61·5	102·5	61·5	102·5
Wage bill	62	62	62	62	62	62	63·2	63·2
Outside purchases (value)	20	20	20	20	20·5	20·5	20·5	20·5
VAT payable	—	—	1	2	1	2	1	2
Base of corporation tax	18	18	17	16	18	18	16·8	16·8
Corporation tax	8·1	8·1	6·8	6·4	7·2	7·2	6·7	6·7
Profits after tax	9·9	9·9	10·2	9·6	10·8	10·8	10·1	10·1
Change in total tax paid	—	—	−0·3	+0·3	+0·1	+1·1	−0·4	+0·6
Wages/profits after tax	6·26		6·26		5·74		6·26	
Ratio of A's net profits to B's net profits	1·0		1·06		1·0		1·0	

* It is assumed that export prices are fixed by world market forces.

absorbed. This is the most favourable assumption for the effect of the introduction of a VAT on the balance of payments. It is a situation that might be approached if one supposed firms like firm A in example 1 to be generally the price leaders in their respective industries. In this case, since corporation tax is levied on total profits, regardless of the distribution of the production out of which those profits arise between foreign and home markets while the VAT, on the other hand, is levied on value added *in sales to the domestic market alone*, the burden of tax is shifted towards firm B which has no stake in the export market, whose taxable value added is 80/120 of the combined value added of the two firms, and who therefore pays twice the VAT that B pays. The ratio of the profits of the two firms after corporation tax at 40 per cent has changed from 1 to 1·06. After-tax profits of A increase by 0·3; B's decrease by the same amount.

5.89 As in example 1, it would appear that A might, with advantage, seek to absorb the VAT on the home market, making it difficult for B to maintain its profitability except by seeking to make sales overseas as well. The switch of emphasis in the tax system, slightly away from country-of-origin taxes on profits towards the VAT (a country-of-destination indirect tax on domestic consumption alone) would seem to encourage both firms to seek to export more, since it changes the relative profitability, after tax, of home and export sales. The circumstances in which this would *not* be so are those described in columns 3 and 4; (these, it may be noted, are the circumstances in which a currency *devaluation*, also, would provide no export benefit or incentive). Here, it is assumed that home prices can rise freely by the full amount of the VAT, while the price of exports, because of international competition, cannot be raised. In that event, firm B, with its higher ratio of domestic sales to exports, is exactly compensated for its higher burden of VAT by the increase in home market prices. The pricing policy in the home market that this assumes is one that actually *increases* the after-tax profits of both firms by about 9 per cent; and some might think that the full and automatic shifting of the VAT is not therefore altogether plausible. In column 4, an upward adjustment of wages is assumed, to retain the original income distribution and to match the general $2\frac{1}{2}$ per cent increase in domestic prices assumed in column 3. Since both firms have the same wage bill, the relative profitability of the two firms is unaffected by this further change.

Example 3

5.90 In example 3, for simplicity, purchases are taken to be solely capital purchases for replacement purposes, and it is assumed that one-tenth of the capital stock of each firm requires to be replaced each 'year'. The sales of the two firms are again the same, and the average rate of return on capital of each firm is initially the same (column 1) before a VAT is introduced. The ratio of capital to output in firm A is twice that in firm B, and so its profit margin on *sales* is also twice that of B. The rate of return on capital, net of corporation tax, is $5\frac{1}{2}$ per cent for each firm. In contrast to the two earlier examples, we now consider the accounts of these two firms after a 5 per cent VAT is introduced, *without* any offsetting reduction in the corporation tax. This is a different kind of tax change, and one that would be much less likely to benefit exports, since a general increase in domestic costs and prices would seem almost inevitable. It is here assumed, in fact, that all prices, including the prices of replacement capital goods and asset valuations, increase by the full 5 per cent. The example serves to show that, *in certain circumstances*, at least one possible effect of a VAT—ie its discrimination in favour of the capital-intensive firm—does not depend upon a corresponding reduction in the corporation tax.

5.91 In column 2, no such discrimination results; since it is assumed that money wages do not change, the two firms are in the same boat. Each adds to its invoices VAT of 5 units on its sales, and each also pays an additional 5, either in VAT or in the tax invoiced to it in its purchase of replacement assets. The distribution of its total revenue between taxable value added and replacement purchase is immaterial. The average rate of return of each firm on its fixed capital at replacement cost valuation falls, as a result of the uncompensated VAT, to $5\frac{1}{4}$ per cent. However, it seems plausible that, if all prices rise by 5 per cent, there will, in the final analysis, be some rise

Example 3 A is more capital intensive than B (initial rates of profit on capital are equal)

| | (1) 45% corporation tax; nil VAT | | 45% corporation tax; 5% VAT; 5% increase in all goods prices, including capital goods | | | | | |
| | | | (2) No increase in wages | | (3) $2\frac{1}{2}$% increase in wages | | (4) 5% increase in wages | |
	A	B	A	B	A	B	A	B
Sales net of VAT	100	100	100	100	100	100	100	100
Sales including VAT	—	—	105	105	105	105	105	105
Replacement cost depreciation	40	20	40	20	40	20	40	20
Replacement cost depreciation including VAT	—	—	42	21	42	21	42	21
Wage bill	20	60	20	60	20·5	61·5	21	63
VAT on final sales	—	—	5	5	5	5	5	5
Less VAT invoiced on purchases	—	—	−2	−1	−2	−1	−2	−1
VAT chargeable to these firms	—	—	3	4	3	4	3	4
Total costs (including VAT)	60	80	65	85	65·5	86·5	66	88
Base of corporation tax	40	20	40	20	39·5	18·5	39	17
Corporation tax	18	9	18	9	17·8	8·3	17·5	7·7
Profit after tax	22	11	22	11	21·7	10·2	21·5	9·3
% Return on capital after tax (Capital is assumed to equal 10 times replacement cost depreciation)	5·5	5·5	5·24	5·24	5·2	4·9	5·1	4·4

in money wage rates as well. In columns 3 and 4, two sample possibilities are considered: a rise in wages of $2\frac{1}{2}$ per cent and a rise in wages in proportion to the 5 per cent increase in prices induced by the VAT. These cases drive a wedge between the more and the less capital-intensive firm. The two firms differ, quite simply, in one respect: the size of their respective wage bills. To a larger extent than A, firm B is, in effect, 'paying' the VAT twice over: first, in the price of its replacement investment purchases, and its own taxable value added; and *secondly* in its wages, which reflect the influence of the VAT on the general price level. In column 3, B's net rate of return on capital is 4·9 per cent and A's 5·2 per cent. In column 4, B's is 4·4 per cent and A's 5·1 per cent. Had there also been a compensating reduction in the rate of corporation tax, A's rate of return would have been higher, and B's lower than originally.

5.92 In general, the only circumstances in which the more capital-intensive firm would not be advantaged would be when the *difference* between the consequent increase in prices (including the prices of capital goods) and the consequent increase in money wages, resulting from the imposition of a VAT, was as much as, or greater than, the VAT itself. It may be doubted whether such circumstances would be consistent with full employment and the existing mechanisms for determining wages.

Annex 2

**The possibility of
basing VAT on
purchase tax**

5.93 In a VAT system there is no reason, in principle, why certain purchases
should not be made at early stages of the productive process while allowing
the payment of the tax on value added to be postponed to a later stage:
for example until the wholesale stage. On one view, our present purchase
tax system is very close to this situation up to the wholesale stage, with
purchases at earlier stages being made 'under suspension of the tax'.
If a VAT were introduced and administered in such a way that suspension
of tax operated *universally* up to the wholesale stage, then up to that point
it would be indistinguishable from a universal purchase tax. For example
in Chapter 2 (Table 1 in paragraph 2.9) it will be seen that at the
wholesale stage the VAT liability is 25 (ie 10 per cent of 250, the selling
price). It is the fact that 20 of this has already been paid at previous stages
which entitles the wholesaler to a credit, making *his* actual tax payment
only 5. If the previous payments of tax were suspended, of course, the
credits would not arise, and the wholesaler would be liable to the whole
amount of 25, as under purchase tax at present.

5.94 A piecemeal implementation of such tax suspension would, however, be
unworkable, since credits for tax invoiced on purchases could only be
allowed in respect of sales on which tax had been paid, ie, *not* on sales made
under suspension of tax. Given the complex network of commercial
transactions it is certain that at least some, and probably many, sales would
fall into the latter category. Certain transactions 'under suspension of tax',
with the tax accumulated and postponed to a later stage, are, nevertheless,
provided for in French VAT legislation. The Dutch VAT law also provides
for the deferment of VAT due on imports where these are purchased by a
trader, until the trader makes a sale either of the import or of a product
incorporating it.

5.95 However, despite these cases, and although it is interesting to consider
whether a VAT could be built on to the existing purchase tax, it is not clear
that large scale suspension of tax at earlier stages would be consistent with
the EEC directives on VAT. Article 13 of the Second Directive states:
'if a Member State considers that, in exceptional cases, it would be advisable
to adopt special measures so as to simplify collection of the tax or to prevent
certain frauds, it is to inform the Commission and the other Member
States . . . the Council is to decide . . . on the deviation requested . . . (and)
as to the length of application of such measures . . .'. However, in the context
of other parts of the Directives, it seems questionable whether a general
suspension up to the wholesale stage would be permitted by the rules as
they stand, which specify a fractional payments system with tax invoicing
at every stage, and certainly such measures could not survive the transition
to full tax harmonisation.

5.96 If, nevertheless, an attempt was made to make the present purchase tax
the *basis* of a more comprehensive VAT system, it would be necessary to

graft on to it arrangements for the tax treatment of value added at the retail stage, and value added in services, as well as to increase the coverage of taxable goods. A part of the value added in final consumer expenditure arises in the retail distribution of goods and in the provision of services to final consumers which would escape turnover taxation even if purchase tax were extended to cover all goods*. It would, therefore, be necessary to go beyond this if the universal basis of a VAT were to be achieved.

5.97 The first possibility would be to apply a VAT to retailers, using the invoicing system. Consider, for example, a sale from a registered manufacturer or wholesaler direct to a retailer. The former would be liable to pay the purchase tax due, which would be passed on in the price to the latter, but would be shown in the invoice. The retailer would be liable to pay tax on the invoiced value of *his* sales, but would be in credit in respect of the purchase tax which had been passed on to him. If all retail sales were to final consumers the resulting two-stage tax would be equivalent in many respects to a comprehensive VAT. However, sales by retailers back to registered businesses who sell to other registered businesses could give rise to double taxation (and hence discrimination against retail sales to businesses). This is because the registered business, not itself subject to tax, would be in the same position as the tax-exempt firm described in Chapter 2, ie unable to claim a tax credit.

---

* *The purchase tax system, with suspension of tax on transfers of goods 'under representation' between registered businesses is fully described in the Richardson Report, Chapter 4, particularly paragraphs 68–76.*

Table 14

	Purchases		Sales		Tax due	Value added
	Excluding tax	Including tax	Excluding tax	Including tax		
Producer A to Producer B†	—	—	50	50	0	50
Producer A to Retailer C	—	—	100	110	10	100
Retailer C to Producer B	100	110	150	165*	5	50
Producer B to Wholesaler†	—	215	315	315	0	100
Wholesaler to Retailer C	—	315	365	401·5	36·5	50
Retailer C to Final Consumer	365	401·5	415	456·5	5	50
					56·5	400

The appropriate tax here is 40 = 10 per cent of 400.

* Actual tax is greater by 16·5, ie by 10 per cent of the sales back from retailers to registered businesses.

† Untaxed transaction stages.

5.98 This situation is illustrated in Table 14, which shows how that part of total value added in final consumption which is represented by sales back from retailer to registered businesses is subject to double taxation (assuming 10 per cent purchase tax and 10 per cent retail VAT).

5.99 An alternative arrangement would be to apply a retail stage VAT as outlined above, but to allow to the registered business purchaser from an unregistered retailer a cash refund of the taxes levied and invoiced at the purchase tax and retail VAT stages. (Sales to businesses by retailers 'under representation' would not remove double taxation: they would only free producer goods from tax on retail value added, not from the purchase tax as well.) The effect of this would be to change the bottom three rows of the preceding table, as shown in Table 15.

Table 15

	Purchases		Sales		Tax due	Value added
	Excluding tax	Including tax	Excluding tax	Including tax		
Producer B to Wholesaler	200	215	300	300	−15	100
Wholesaler to Retailer C	—	300	350	385	35	50
Retailer C to Final Consumer	350	385	400	440	5	50
					40	400

5.100 Since this scheme would require all producers who make retail purchases and who wish to claim tax credits to present verifiable statements of these purchases, it is unlikely that attempting to make indirect taxation comprehensive and non-discriminatory in this way would offer administrative savings compared with a fully fractional VAT system. It may be seen that no producer-to-producer, producer-to-wholesaler or wholesaler-to-producer transfer of goods would need to be invoiced for tax. Compared with the burden of administering an extended single-stage purchase tax, the extra burden of extending taxation to the retail stage in a way which avoids all possibility of double taxation lies in the levying of tax on all retail sales less credits for purchase tax, and in the proper invoicing of these sales when they are made back to registered businesses or from one retailer to another.

5.101 The levying of tax at the retail stage is of course one of the most difficult problems involved in the introduction of a VAT, and it is, therefore, very unlikely in practice that this method of assimilating purchase tax into a more broadly based system would be adopted. Far more likely would be the extension of purchase tax at the wholesale stage to all goods, with perhaps a simplification of the system of rates, with the taxation of services being dealt with separately, eg by SET. Subsequently the earlier stages of production could be brought into the system if the device of fractional collection were desired.

Industrial views 6

6.1 In preparing its report on turnover taxation, the Richardson Committee conducted an enquiry to ascertain the views of industry on the effects of replacing profits tax by a value added tax on prices, exports and imports, investment, business efficiency and on different types of firm. The enquiry took the form of a questionnaire* addressed to 17 business organisations, 14 of them being large firms in the private sector and three being nationalised industries. These organisations also gave oral evidence. In general, the evidence confirmed the views of the Richardson Committee that the economic advantages which had been claimed for a tax switch of this kind were unlikely to be achieved, principally because the industrialists regarded a value added tax and profits tax as being very different from one another: in particular, they took the view that profits tax did not affect their pricing policy. In other words a cut in profits tax would not reduce prices, while the substitution of a value added tax would certainly raise them. This would weaken or destroy the case that exports and investment would be encouraged by such a tax switch (see Chapter 5, paragraphs 5.31 et seq).

6.2 For the purposes of this present enquiry it was felt necessary to make a further approach to industry in order to obtain its views on the issue. There were a number of reasons for this. Firstly, the firms whose views were sought by the Richardson Committee were relatively few in number, and were all very large. Secondly, the question put to these firms related only to the effects of a switch from profits tax to VAT. Thirdly, it was thought that the passage of time might have altered the economic environment sufficiently to modify or qualify some of the earlier answers: in particular the growing use of more sophisticated accounting processes and the increasingly competitive trading climate might have altered the situation so far as pricing behaviour was concerned. In order to make this approach it was felt that the widely spread network of Economic Development Committees (EDCs) would be a valuable instrument to use, and accordingly a questionnaire with a certain amount of explanatory material, was circulated to them.

6.3 Five basic questions were asked:
 a Which of the two methods of administering a VAT (ie the 'accounts' method or the 'invoicing' method) appears most advantageous?
 b What would be the effect on the pricing policy of the industry concerned of a switch from corporation tax to an equal yielding VAT; say, $1\frac{1}{4}$ per cent VAT for a 5 per cent reduction in corporation tax or a $2\frac{1}{2}$ per cent VAT for a 10 per cent cut in corporation tax; what would be the effect on exports, investment and efficiency?
 c What would be the effect on the industry of the substitution of a VAT for purchase tax and the selective employment tax?

See Appendix F of the Report of the Richardson Committee.

d What are the industry's views on the general issue of extending the base of indirect taxation, either by selective extensions into the field of untaxed consumer expenditure, or by a more broadly based tax such as VAT?

e What general comments does the industry have on the broader taxation questions raised by the possible introduction of a VAT?

6.4 Quite clearly there are a number of problems raised by any questionnaire of this kind. The impact of the actual introduction of a VAT on industry would depend almost entirely on the rates and coverage of the tax, and the taxes for which it was substituted or which were consequently modified. None of these factors could be known and the questions posed were therefore inevitably hypothetical. In particular, for example, the notion of a $1\frac{1}{4}$ or $2\frac{1}{2}$ per cent VAT (see item 2 above) is somewhat unrealistic, but, since it appeared that a reduction of more than 5 or 10 percentage points in corporation tax would not be a practical proposition, it was necessary, in order to isolate the possible effects of this switch, to work on the basis of an equal yield switch from the one tax to the other and on the assumption that all else remained unchanged. It was, however, pointed out to the EDCs that, in practical terms, a substantially higher rate of VAT was more likely and that therefore there were a number of possible tax switches and combinations which might be envisaged. It was illustratively suggested, for example, that (on the basis of the tax rates prevailing in the Spring of 1968, though these were subsequently raised substantially in the Budget) a basic rate of VAT on all expenditure of about 7 per cent (with some higher and lower rates) could just about replace the revenue lost to the Government by a 5 per cent cut in corporation tax, and the abolition of purchase tax and SET. It was, however, further pointed out that VAT rates at this level would be substantially lower than those prevailing in Europe, and of course the big increases in SET and purchase tax in the 1968 and 1969 Budgets would have raised the equal yielding VAT rate to over 10 per cent.

6.5 The EDCs responses to these questions are probably best regarded as mainly, though not exclusively, a consensus of the views of the management side of the industry. While the trade union representatives often participated in the discussions of the EDCs, or of the special working groups which were set up, it was felt that the nature of the questions which were asked, ie on the effects of VAT on costs and pricing policy, made them primarily a matter for management, and the unions, therefore, reserved their position on these questions although they were naturally concerned with the overall economic implication of the possible tax change.

6.6 A full summary of the EDCs views is contained in the Appendix, but here it may be noted that their replies were, as might be expected, very diverse, and only on a few matters did a clear majority view emerge. There was. for example, no clear majority support for the VAT on its own merits as a substitute for part of the corporation tax, and/or for the purchase tax and the SET. Similarly, there was no clear majority support, and some strong opposition, to the VAT as a method of widening the base of British taxation. Cautions were common that the Government should take a decision on whether or not to introduce a VAT only after a full and careful investigation of its social and administrative implications. At the same time it was widely felt that the VAT would have to be introduced into Britain in due course if the country entered the EEC.

6.7 The conclusions of the EDCs on the question of the effects of a substitution of the VAT for part of the corporation tax generally ran counter to those of the Richardson Committee, though not strongly so. In many markets it was felt by the majority of EDCs that competition would be keen enough to ensure that the reduction of corporation tax would be taken into account and would lead to a lowering of prices, even though, as it was widely (not quite unanimously) agreed, the VAT is a tax which, in itself, businessmen would pass on as readily as they now do other indirect taxes. Many businessmen, especially in the most progressive companies which are often their industry's price-leaders, take account of after-tax rates of return on capital in deciding on pricing and long term investment policies. Thus in the view of these EDCs a reduction in the level of corporation tax could stimulate investment and lead eventually to lower real prices, provided that (and this point found frequent emphasis) it was a significant reduction of at least 5 and perhaps even 10 percentage points.

6.8 Nevertheless, and alongside these opinions, there were widespread doubts about whether the stimulus to investment would be of much practical significance. These doubts were even more general (though by no means universal) about the stimulus which the tax changes would give to ways of seeking to cut costs.

6.9 The EDCs generally also shared the Richardson Committee's fears that the inflationary consequences of the tax change, through higher prices and wages, would quickly erode the benefits it might bring to exports and firms in competition with imports. Even if the erosion were not complete there was considerable pessimism as to whether the tax change would bring about much import-saving. There was more optimism about the effect on exports, given favourable assumptions about movements in other prices and costs.

6.10 The administrative costs to industry as well as for the Government was the most commonly expressed objection or reservation to the VAT. These costs were perhaps most frequently commented on by the EDCs when they compared the implications of a multi-stage VAT with the single-stage purchase tax and the SET.

6.11 Strong objections to the SET were widely expressed, but some EDCs stated that their industries would be relatively worse off if a VAT were substituted for it, and there was no attempt to justify a VAT solely as a substitute for the SET.

6.12 Although it was fairly widely recognised that differential rates of tax were likely if a VAT were introduced, and the taxation of food at a low or 'nil-rate' was the most widely mentioned example, there were some definite preferences on grounds of simplicity of administration and avoidance of 'arbitrariness' for a single, uniform, comprehensive rate. If differential rates were inevitable, the EDCs in general clearly preferred that their range should be as narrow as possible. At the same time there was recognition that, just as a VAT could have differential rates like the present purchase tax, an extended purchase tax could, if required, be modified so that it would be levied on a more uniform basis, and with smaller changes in rates when adjustments were required to regulate domestic demand.

6.13 A majority of the EDCs favoured administering the VAT by the invoicing rather than the accounts method, the main reasons being that this method was used in the EEC, and also the expectation that any VAT introduced in the UK would be levied at differential rates. Nevertheless there were some definite opinions in favour of the accounts method, particularly if invoicing is not mandatory on EEC members, and if the Government was prepared to take the political decision of introducing the VAT at a single uniform comprehensive rate. Some EDCs argued that the accounts method would pose fewer administrative problems than the invoicing method to the many small firms in their industries. Others argued that neither method would be suitable for such businesses, and that some special tax would be necessary.

6.14 To sum up, therefore, it is clear that there is no unanimity in industrial circles as to the merits or demerits of introducing a VAT in the UK. There are, of course, widespread views in industry that many tax rates in the UK are 'too high' or that aspects of the system are 'too complicated', although generalities such as these were not frequently expressed in the EDCs replies. What was very clear, however, was the feeling that if a VAT were to be introduced it should be done on the simplest possible basis and that it should provide the opportunity for a re-examination of the tax system as a whole.

Appendix: Summary of replies to the industrial questionnaire

A.1 In 1968/69 a questionnaire and explanatory paper prepared by the National Economic Development Office directed the attention of the EDCs to the possibility that a VAT might be seen as a substitute for a part of corporation tax, thus covering similar ground to that dealt with by the Richardson Committee in 1964. In addition the EDCs were asked to consider the implications for their industries of using a VAT as an alternative to purchase tax and/or SET.

A.2 The handling of this enquiry was carried out differently from one EDC to another, but replies, often with extensive memoranda and detailed analysis, were received from the EDCs for:
Agriculture
Building   ⎫
Civil Engineering ⎬ Joint Report
Chemicals
Clothing
Distributive Trades
Electrical Engineering
Electronics
Food Manufacturing*
Hosiery and Knitwear*
Hotel and Catering
Machine Tools   ⎫
Mechanical Engineering ⎬ Joint Report
Motor Manufacturing
Motor Vehicle Distribution and Repair
Paper and Board*
Post Office*
Printing and Publishing
Rubber*
Wool Textiles
In addition a memorandum was received from the Oil Industry Taxation Committee.

The nature of the enquiry A.3 The questions put to the EDCs in inviting their views on the consequences of a VAT, particularly for their own industries, covered the main topics with which the Richardson Committee dealt, namely the possibility of introducing a VAT as a substitute for the purchase tax and a part of the corporation tax (then income and profits tax). It was felt that the EDCs, with access to the well informed views of a cross section of industrial opinion, had a uniquely valuable contribution to make to the re-examination of the Richardson Committee's conclusions against the economic arguments which had been advanced for these substitutions. The questionnaire to the EDCs, however,

* *These EDCs have since been wound up.*

90

also raised three other topics:

a The substitution of VAT for the SET (which did not exist when the Richardson Committee reported)

b The alleged way in which the VAT would favour producers with high ratios of capital to labour as compared with producers with low ratios, even though the corporation tax were unchanged

c The general merits of the VAT as a way of extending the base of indirect taxation.

The memorandum which was sent to the EDCs was not, however, simply a list of questions: it was more of a discussion paper. It outlined the arguments for the VAT, presented numerical illustrations of them, made some illustrative assumptions about possible rates and coverage of the tax, and observations about its possible form.

A.4 The central observation was the need for the EDCs to take into account that:

a The introduction of a VAT would represent a major change in the British tax structure

b It would involve considerable administrative problems

c It is capable of yielding very large sums in revenue

d If Britain becomes a member of the EEC, tax rates as well as tax systems would be harmonised in due course.

A.5 The main requirement was, however, for the VAT to be considered on its merits and not simply as a requirement of Common Market membership. It was also suggested that the present policy of levying different rates of indirect taxation on different items of consumption would be likely to continue even with a VAT.

The nature of the replies A.6 The questionnaire was considered in a variety of different ways, but generally in detail by special working groups of the EDCs. Two pairs of EDCs (Building and Civil Engineering; and Mechanical Engineering and Machine Tools) had joint working groups. The replies were formulated usually, though not in a systematic or in a uniform manner, in consultation with firms and trade associations in the industries concerned. For example, the Chemicals EDC circulated its first report to 'forty-one firms of the Chemical Industries Association, broadly representative of all manufacturing activities within its industry, and to eighteen trade associations with specialised interests . . .'. The construction industry's report was prepared by NEDO staff who 'consulted leading economists in the industry, and circulated a paper to all the main trade associations, professional institutions and trade unions for their comments'. The industry's EDC transmitted the group's paper to the VAT Committee on the understanding that the industry would be further consulted if legislation were contemplated. The chairman of the Electrical Engineering EDC circulated a letter, not only to the management members of his EDC, but to several other chief executives in his industry.

The Motor Vehicle Distribution and Repair E D C's report incorporated views of individual members of the Motor Agents Association's National Vehicle Committee. Respondents to a questionnaire from the Hotel and Catering E D C . . . 'covered the main sectors of the industry, hotels, catering establishments and public houses . . . (which) . . . although . . . not a cross-section of the industry . . . (were) . . . indicative of the likely effect of a V A T on the industry as a whole.' The British Rubber Manufacturers' Association was responsible for the report on behalf of the Rubber Industry E D C. In three industries (electrical engineering/electronics, motor manufacturing and the oil industry) permanent working parties already exist to consider tax matters, and the reports of the British Electrical and Allied Manufacturers' Association (B E A M A) Taxation Panel, and the Taxation Panel of the S M M T and the Oil Industry Taxation Committee are integral parts of the reports of the E D Cs and of the industry concerned. The report of the Printing and Publishing E D C summarised separately the views of each section of its industry (newspapers, printing and book publishing) because of their diversity.

A.7 Apart from the general reservations of the trade union members, which were primarily concerned with doubts about the general balance of direct and indirect taxation and concern over the possible effects on income distribution, the reports were not always unanimous. Members of the Electronics E D C recorded notes of dissent with, and differences of emphasis from, the B E A M A Taxation Panel. An employer member of the Wool Textiles E D C also submitted an individual memorandum. The Government departmental members also had to reserve their positions. For example, the Food Manufacturing E D C prefaces its report with the comment '. . . departmental members have participated most helpfully in discussion and have influenced the answers, . . . in references to . . . S E T the Government members wish to remain uncommitted to the general view'.

A.8 This account is, therefore, best regarded as primarily a summary of the views of the management sides of the E D Cs, formed and modified in the light of the observations of other industrialists and managers in their industries, and of their trade union and departmental colleagues. Not all the reports (eg those of Mechanical Engineering, Printing and Publishing, Paper and Board) were considered by full meetings of the E D Cs concerned.

General attitudes to the VAT

a) Reorganisation of British taxation

A.9 There was wide agreement amongst the E D Cs that if a V A T is introduced, it should be part of a general reorganisation and simplification of British taxation. Some of the changes envisaged were often, and in the context of the enquiry rightly, those particularly beneficial to the E D C's industry. The Distributive Trades E D C thought that retailers, whom it found as a group opposed to the V A T, might be reconciled to the tax if its introduction resulted in the abolition of the discrimination against distributors in the administration of S E T, R E P, investment grants and depreciation allowances on buildings as well as in a reduction in the personal taxation of individuals. There could be nothing but 'dismay at the prospect of an additional tax . . .'. The E D C also recognised the serious implications of a V A T for social policy.

A.10 The SMMT Taxation Panel supported a broadly based V A T with narrow differentials, provided that it superseded the purchase tax and enabled the corporation tax to be reduced by at least 5 per cent, though it recognised that the features of the purchase tax which it finds most objectionable—namely the high rate on its own industry's products and the frequency with which those rates are changed—did not require for their remedy the substitution of a V A T for the purchase tax.

A.11 The Clothing E D C, which saw no particular advantage and much additional trouble and expense in substituting the V A T for the purchase tax, S E T and part of the corporation tax, added that 'any change would therefore only seem worthwhile if it resulted in a general simplification of the tax structure'.

A.12 The Food Manufacturing, Rubber and Electronics E D Cs also thought that a V A T could only be sensibly considered as part of a radical reorganisation of taxation including, in the Rubber and Food Manufacturing E D Cs' view, personal taxation, and in the view of the Electronics E D C 'possibly the R E P' and the financing of social security 'so as to emphasise the true cost of labour and so strengthen the incentives to labour efficiently'. The Wool Textile E D C looked upon the V A T primarily as a substitute for other forms of taxation. 'No form of taxation can be regarded as an incentive to industry'. The Construction E D Cs' views were that a V A T would be a benefit to their industries only if it led to 'a substantial reduction in . . . corporation tax *and*, "since so many building firms are unincorporated or close companies", in personal income tax.' The Post Office thought it unrealistic to envisage a V A T at less than 10 per cent which they considered would, at present rates, be enough to replace the purchase tax, S E T and a small part of the corporation tax and perhaps leave room for other switches and simplifications.

A.13 While the BEAMA Taxation Panel saw the V A T as offering the possibility of an overhauling of British taxation with the abolition of S E T, the purchase tax and substantial cuts in other indirect taxes and in the corporation tax, it nevertheless thought a more widely based purchase tax could achieve some of the objectives claimed for a V A T.

b) The taxation of food

A.14 The Food Manufacturing and Agriculture E D Cs, appropriately enough, commented that the general taxation of food, which is likely to be involved in a V A T, would be '. . . contrary to long established practice of British Governments and with profound social implications', (Food Manufacturing) and 'a major departure from century-old principles' (Agriculture). Indeed, the Agriculture E D C was in outright opposition to the tax for reasons taken up in the next section. The SMMT Panel also observed that, in general, the decision to introduce a VAT would depend more on political considerations than on the economic pros and cons.

A.15 Because, amongst other reasons, it was thought that food would be likely to fall under a VAT, differential rates were widely regarded as inevitable in the British context—in line also with most Continental experience (Distribution, Motor Manufacturing, Food Manufacturing, Rubber). Nevertheless, the Distribution, Chemicals, Motor Manufacturing, Motor Vehicle Distribution and Repair and Food Manufacturing EDCs hoped that the differentials would be kept to a minimum.

c) Further possible studies

A.16 The application of the VAT to retailers raises many problems, and the Distributive Trades EDC urged that it was vital for the Government, if contemplating the introduction of VAT, to examine closely the problems which the extension of the VAT to retailers raises in the EEC. The Mechanical Engineering EDC also urged the importance of learning from Continental experience, particularly what problems the German Government had met in introducing a VAT in January 1968. The Construction report suggested that it might be 'useful to examine the impact of the VAT on professional partnerships, like architects and consulting engineers'. A different kind of study is implied by the importance which the Motor Manufacturing EDC attaches to its industry's being consulted by the Government 'so that it can play a positive role in the formulation of policy on the administration of a VAT system to its industry'. And still another kind of study would be involved if the Clothing EDC's recommendation were followed up that the social consequences of a VAT be subjected to a separate enquiry before any decision is taken on the tax.

Special problems of the VAT for individual industries

A.17 Some EDCs gave special attention to the problems which a VAT would raise for their industries. The Distributive Trades EDC was concerned about retailers, many of whom are in a small way of business and whose records are often inadequate. Not only did this EDC urge a special study of Continental experience, but it also thought that special arrangements under the VAT would probably be necessary for taxing retailers with small turnovers. (Perhaps a sales tax at a low rate without entitlement to rebate of the VAT paid on purchases.) A similar point was made on behalf of the construction industry which has no less than 57,500 firms which employ less than eight operatives. Timing the introduction of a VAT should also have regard to the special problems which decimalisation, and further metrication, will pose for retailers—a group pre-eminently in direct contact with the public. Major changes should come 'one at a time'. Indeed, the EDC 'earnestly recommended that any move to a VAT should not take place in the period 1971/76'. The Distributive Trades EDC's view on timing the introduction of the VAT in relation to decimalisation was supported by the SMMT Taxation Committee and by the Mechanical Engineering EDC.

A.18 The Post Office EDC stressed the case for exempting its services from a VAT as is already done in France and Germany, and is proposed in the Netherlands. (In Denmark telecommunications only are exempt.) It also discussed the two possible methods of doing this: the 'normal' and 'nil-rate' methods. Under the 'normal' method, though the Post Office would not itself be liable to charge VAT on its sales, neither would it receive credit for the VAT it had paid on its purchases from other businesses. If its VAT inclusive costs rose and, to recoup the increases, it raised its own charges, it would in effect be passing on to its customers the VAT on its purchases but not in the formal way (eg on invoices) which would enable its business customers to rebate the tax already paid against their own VAT liabilities. These businesses would as a consequence suffer some 'cumulation' of the VAT. In contrast, under the 'nil-rate' method, exempt institutions are rebated the VAT they have paid on supplies and this would eliminate the direct effects of the VAT on the Post Office's costs. The Dutch Government was believed to be proposing to make use of nil-rates, though not for postal and telecommunications services. The EEC's Second Directive on the VAT, however, limits the use of nil-rates to the current transitional period.

A.19 The possible exemption from the VAT of its industry's suppliers of fuel and energy was a matter of concern to the Chemical Industry's EDC. If these suppliers passed on the VAT which had been included in their costs, 'normal' exemption would result in the chemical industry's falling foul of the 'cumulation' of the VAT just described—to the detriment of its international competitiveness. The EDC would prefer fuel and energy to be liable to the VAT rather than its exports should suffer this spill-over. It would regard the introduction of a VAT as an opportunity for the Government to eliminate the spill-over on to the cost of exports of the present duty on fuel oil, not as an occasion for exacerbating the problem.

A.20 The UK Oil Industry Taxation Committee reported their fears lest a VAT should be charged on oils but not on competing (nationalised) sources of fuel and power. It pointed out that the large proportion of imports in the value of output in the oil industry meant that a VAT would be largely reflected in prices, except to the extent that there were any offsetting reduction in the hydro-carbon oil duties. It hoped that a VAT would be thought of as an alternative to part of the oil duties rather than as an additional burden imposed on a value which included existing duties. This latter point (the tax falling on the price including duty) was felt to be a strong reason for the application of a reduced rate (as in the Netherlands and France). As between specific duties and a VAT, a VAT was preferred on the grounds of its greater neutrality between industries.

A.21 A central concern of the Agriculture EDC stemmed from its contention that, if a VAT were imposed on its industry, the tax-exclusive prices of much of its industry's output would actually be reduced because the VAT on many imported products would be absorbed by overseas suppliers. While this problem might be dealt with in a number of ways, the EDC strongly favoured the application to farmers of the nil-rate system.* It was not enough to exempt farm sales without payment of refunds as this would give an impetus to self-sufficiency amongst farmers and cut across the current trend to greater specialisation which has contributed so much to increased agricultural efficiency in recent years. Under EEC regulations, farm sales are either exempt from the VAT or liable at a reduced rate. The Agriculture EDC was also concerned, like the Distributive Trades EDC, with what the VAT would mean for small businesses.

A.22 The construction report drew attention to three special problems. First, like the report from the Distributive Trades EDC, it noted the very large number of small firms in its industry which would, because of their 'primitive accountancy', find it difficult to cope with a VAT. Secondly, though the products of many industries are purchased by public bodies—such as hospital boards and local authorities—as well as by private businesses, it was this report, largely because about half of new construction is purchased by such bodies, which raised an important implication of this. Public bodies (as distinct from any 'industrial' establishments which they control) will almost certainly not pay VAT directly, so, under the tax, a local authority, for example, which purchases a new office (say) would not be able to rebate the VAT element in the cost of this 'capital good' as would a private business subject to the VAT. The Government must, in one way or another, face up to this. The third problem stems from the 'essentiality' of new houses. This has led other governments to give them special treatment under their VATs. For example, a Swedish Committee has recommended that their country's proposed VAT be levied on 60 per cent, not 100 per cent, of a new house's value. In Britain the emphasis of current housing policy is increasingly on 'improvements'. If these (and repairs and maintenance) have to bear a VAT fully, special treatment of new housing would run counter to current policy. New housing has not been specially treated under the SET, and the construction report prefers this principle for a VAT.

A.23 The Hotel and Catering EDC 'obtained information on the application of the VAT to hotels and restaurants in France . . . and . . . gave particular consideration to a report by the VAT study group of the Centre for Study and Promotion of the French Hotel Industry'. One conclusion to emerge was

---

* This was the system originally proposed by the Dutch. The effect would be to treat agriculture in the same way as exports, ie to permit the recovery of tax invoiced on purchases by the industry even though it is exempted from tax on its sales. It is the limiting case of the application of a reduced rate of VAT.

that the French Government had set the limit of exemption from the VAT too low to relieve adequately the very great accounting and administrative difficulties which the tax raises for small firms and establishments. The EDC noted the precedent set in Britain by the exemption from the Hotel and Catering Industrial Training Board Levy of all establishments whose annual pay roll was under £4,000, '. . . . as a result only 11,000 establishments out of 140,000 pay the levy'. For the larger establishments which are a substantial part of the total trade the EDC commended the new French method of assisting investment by hotels and catering establishments. Before January 1968 this assistance took the form of investment grants but since then 'on condition that certain minimum physical standards are attained, a hotel, inn or motel . . . can qualify for a greatly reduced rate of VAT'.

Method of collection A.24 The EDCs were asked whether they thought the 'invoicing' method of collecting the VAT was superior or inferior to the 'accounts' method. (These methods are described in Chapter 2.)

A.25 Opinion was very clearly in favour of the invoicing method in spite of the widespread misgivings about the heavier load of administration which it would impose. (Two members of the Electronics EDC thought that the difficulties of introducing the invoicing method would be so considerable that they disagreed with the BEAMA Taxation Panel that it should be preferred.) A number of reports made the point that the growing computerisation of invoicing in industry would increasingly make the invoicing method easier to cope with. A reason for favouring invoicing was the fairly general expectation, already noted, that a VAT would be levied at differential rates, and it is acknowledged that the accounts method is impracticable if this is done. Several EDCs (eg Chemicals) and the oil industry thought that the issue was definitely pre-judged by the use of the invoicing method in the EEC whether or not the UK decided to levy the VAT at a single rate. 'As we may enter we should avoid the possibility of having to change later' (BEAMA Taxation Panel). The Wool Textiles EDC, which preferred the accounts method (administered through the Inland Revenue's existing tax collecting accounts procedures), presses the Government, before it comes to a decision, to ascertain definitely whether EEC membership would oblige Britain to adopt invoicing, and whether or not the appearance of a direct tax which the accounts method would lend to the VAT made its rebating on exports impermissible under international obligations. The Distributive Trades EDC thought the procedures followed in Germany under that country's VAT deserved study as 'appearing to combine the merits of both invoicing and accounts methods'.

A.26 Two other aspects of the invoicing method were often mentioned as advantageous: its 'self-policing' nature, and its making easier the use of the VAT as a short term regulator of the economy. A disadvantage, mentioned for example by the Food Manufacturing EDC, as compared with the accounts method, was that the more frequent collection of taxes reduced business liquidity.

A.27 A clear recommendation for the accounts method came from the Post Office EDC, 'in spite of the widespread use of the invoicing method on the Continent'. The Motor Vehicle Distribution and Repair EDC also favoured this method if a single rate VAT were imposed and if the obligations of possible EEC membership are not mandatory in favour of invoicing. The Hotel and Catering EDC (though it made no reference to the issue of single or differential rates for the VAT) was another EDC clearly in favour of the accounts method—so long as the procedure involved was comparable to the collection of the corporation tax. The invoicing method would not only be onerous to its industry in relation to sales but also to purchases . . . 'for most establishments in the industry there are a large number of relatively small purchases at fairly frequent intervals'. French experience confirms this: 'the main burden of the VAT there is in analysing and accounting for the tax on purchases'. While the newspaper industry's representatives were divided on the issue, the printers' representatives were still another group who favoured the accounts method because they thought it likely to be administratively cheaper and therefore more acceptable to the many small printers in their industry.

A.28 Similarly the Food Manufacturing EDC envisaged—in line with German practice—a possible role for an accounts method of some kind in levying the VAT on businesses (including small retailers) with less than some specified turnover. It also suggested—so as to avoid the difficulties that *new* firms in particular might otherwise encounter—the adoption of the German procedure of actually paying a firm the refunds of VAT to which it was entitled if, in settling accounts with the tax collector, its liabilities to VAT on its own sales proved insufficient to cancel out its entitlement.

A.29 There was not much support for the argument that under the accounts method a VAT would be less likely to be 'passed on' in higher prices if it were substituted for part of the corporation tax, which is also collected by an accounts method. Such support as there was related to the impact effect of the substitution. There would, in the longer run, be no substantial difference between the two methods of collection in this respect (the Food and Clothing EDCs and the BEAMA Taxation Panel). The SMMT Panel and the Motor Vehicle Distribution and Repair EDC touched on the fear that under the accounts method, where the rebateable VAT is not specifically identified on the invoices which cover purchases, percentage retail margins would be 'marked-up'.

Administrative costs

A.30 The administrative costs which a VAT would impose on industry and the Government, particularly as compared with the purchase tax, and especially if it were extended to retailers, were widely commented on by the EDCs.

Observations by the Hotel and Catering EDC about the difficulties of hotels and restaurants in France under the VAT have already been quoted. It would be necessary for businessmen to keep special accounts, whether or not the VAT were collected by the accounts or invoicing methods (Mechanical Engineering EDC). The administrative costs, which would inevitably be passed on in higher prices, would be so heavy as to rule out any *minor* substitution of the VAT for other taxes (Electrical Engineering EDC). The Clothing EDC saw the administrative costs as the main objection to the VAT, but some other critics saw little to commend the VAT as against the purchase tax, which is not only easier to administer but 'from a social standpoint permits the exemption of essential goods in a way that is not easily done with a VAT'.

A.31 The BEAMA Panel was unanimous that these administrative costs required the most careful preliminary investigation and assessment. This sentiment was shared by the Chemicals EDC. The SMMT Taxation Panel 'feels that it should undertake a study of the practical problems of administering a VAT for discussion with and consideration by NEDO and HMG'.

Richardson re-examined A.32 The conclusions of the Richardson Committee were based mainly on the
a) General committee's interviews of a number of eminent industrialists (see Appendix G of the committee's report, Cmnd 2300), as to how businessmen would respond to a substitution of a VAT for part of the corporation tax and whether the tax-change would stimulate exports, import-saving and efficiency (see Chapters 8 and 9 of the Richardson Report). Specifically to the questions whether:

a Businessmen would offset the fall in corporation tax against the VAT
b A fall in corporation tax would stimulate efficiency, investment and exports
c A VAT would, as an additional impost on imports, encourage import-saving. the Richardson Committee replied negatively.

A.33 As a preliminary, a number of reports (Distributive Trades, Building, Civil Engineering, Food, Agriculture, Hotels and Catering, Clothing and Motor Vehicle Distribution and Repair) drew attention to the fact that many businesses in their industries are unincorporated and would not benefit at all from a reduction in corporation tax. This feature of these industries is naturally important in the interpretation of their EDCs' comments. A necessary counterpart to a cut in corporation tax for these firms would be a cut in personal tax. Another general point which emerged was that the reactions would depend on the size of the substitution. To a marginal substitution the reactions would be similar to those which the Richardson Committee found. A reduction in corporation tax of 5 per cent or less (a reduction of the kind which might be proposed in the course of a normal budget) would not be regarded as permanent and its benefits to investment would be insignificant, its effects on prices probably inflationary

(Distribution, Construction, SMMT Taxation Panel, Motor Vehicle Distribution and Repair and Chemicals). The Mechanical and Electrical Engineering EDCs and the Construction EDCs argued that a 10 per cent reduction in corporation tax was the minimum necessary to have an impact. The Chemicals EDC observed that any substantial cut in corporation tax was unlikely, as contrary to EEC practice. It suggested as an alternative a reduction in the tax on distributions.

A.34 Some industries (and notably the submission of the Oil Industry Committee) pointed out that the change, since Richardson, to corporation tax meant that the impact on prices was likely to be different from that of the old profits tax. If the weight of taxation on corporate profits as a whole, including the income tax paid on company distributions, were reduced if a VAT was introduced, then the net return to the shareholders on their investment would be increased. It is this that the company must consider in assessing the profitability of its projects, given its requirement to raise new equity capital.

A.35 The Food, Distributive Trades and Chemicals EDCs agreed on the extreme unlikelihood of a substantial reduction in corporation tax, both because the rates of the tax are higher abroad, particularly in the EEC, and because of the political pressures on both parties. This judgment was central to the thinking of these EDCs on the tax substitution. The Paper and Board EDC was alone in entering another sort of caveat, at least in respect of prices. A small change ($1\frac{1}{4}$ per cent VAT for 5 per cent corporation tax) might leave prices unaffected; a larger change ($2\frac{1}{2}$ per cent VAT for 10 per cent corporation tax) would not. The oil industry also doubted whether, given the levels of corporation tax ruling in Europe, a reduction was plausible, and made the further point that if a reduction in corporation tax was thought likely to be only *temporary*, it would not be readily reflected in price reductions.

A.36 The Richardson Committee was not without clear support amongst the EDCs. Its arguments were 'cogent and persuasive' to the Wool Textiles EDC. The Motor Vehicle Distribution and Repair EDC was 'in general agreement'. The Clothing EDC (with a qualification about investment) observed that 'business behaviour is likely to be such as not to produce the advantageous effects which are claimed for the tax change'.

A.37 There was agreement with the Richardson Committee on a specific point: the BEAMA Panel agreed that the prices of transport and fuel were likely to increase as a result of the tax change. (It should be noted that if these industries were included in a VAT system but subject to a reduced rate of tax, then the tax on their purchases would be fully recovered, and prices would tend to rise in the absence of any benefit from the reduction of corporation tax, in proportion to the reduced VAT rate.)

A.38 There was agreement with the Richardson Committee that a VAT would be regarded in a different light from a tax on profits. For example, the Printing and Publishing EDC was generally united in broad agreement with the Richardson Committee, and respondents to the Hotel and Catering EDC were also in 'general agreement that their prices would be likely to rise if a VAT were substituted for the corporation tax'. The Distributive Trades EDC believed that the reaction would be to pass on the VAT in prices as a direct element of cost. The Chemicals EDC thought that important suppliers of its industry, the extractive, transport and construction industries (all generally labour-intensive) would pass on the VAT virtually in full and the fall in corporation tax would not be offset against it. Even in the chemicals industry itself ' . . . with its high capital expenditure and substantial exports, the scope . . .' in the short run 'which the average firm would appear to have in absorbing VAT on its home sales, would be very little different from that of the average firm in industry as a whole'. What mainly informed this pessimism was the EDC's belief that a substantial reduction in corporation tax was out of the question. Because of its large capital investment programme, the Post Office has no current or foreseeable liability to corporation tax and if it were made liable to VAT it would have to pass on the tax to maintain its net revenue and hence the net rate of return on its assets. On this basis and on the basis of 1966/67 figures the EDC estimated that a 10 per cent VAT would lead to increases of 7·3 per cent in postal charges and 3·4 per cent in telecommunication charges.

A.39 Nevertheless the consensus amongst the EDCs had a different emphasis from the conclusions of the Richardson Committee. There was more stress on the restraining influence of competition, especially in the long run, and distinctions were drawn between different products according to the circumstances of their markets.

A.40 Even the Clothing EDC, which was pessimistic that the prices might rise by more than the tax because of the low profit margins in its industry and the possibility of cumulation through the application of percentage markups at the retail stage, added that the main influence on prices was the decisions of the price leaders in the industry. In the past, clothing prices have not risen as fast as the average because of 'the competition within the industry'.

A.41 The BEAMA Taxation Panel thought that, in its competitive tendering for long term contracts, its industry would take the reduction in the corporation tax into account quite quickly and that this process could be reinforced by pressure from the Electricity Supply Authorities. It also thought that the retail margins on consumer durables were large enough for some VAT to be absorbed there. Equipment for industry was a different case. Given that their purchasers can rebate the VAT on electrical equipment, the manufacturers of the equipment 'would find it relatively easy to pass on the VAT . . .' The Mechanical Engineering EDC expressed a similar opinion, though in some parts of its industry competitive pressures might bring about (tax-exclusive) price reductions. It must be added that eleven of the thirteen industrialists who submitted opinions to the chairman of the Electrical Engineering EDC 'expected to lose on balance even after taking account of the reduction in corporation tax'.

A.42 The Food Manufacturing EDC stated that though it was 'clear that the VAT would be regarded as an impost to be recovered in selling prices . . . this might be affected by competitive conditions in the industry'. Moreover, pricing decisions are now subject to direct Government intervention. The Wool Textiles EDC, too, thought that competition would prevent prices rising by the full amount of the VAT and so did the Motor Vehicle Distribution and Repair EDC, at least as regards the prices of new cars, and of forecourt services. The prices of second-hand cars broadly follow the prices of new. It is unlikely that this would be true of charges for repairs. Indeed there might be a tendency for the VAT to be 'more than passed on' to recover the tax absorbed on the profits from other activities. This EDC was also particularly concerned about the way in which a VAT might operate in respect of second-hand transactions.

A.43 There was general agreement that price increases resulting from a VAT would lead to wage demands and further price increases. The strength of this process would depend especially on whether the VAT fell on food and the size of any compensatory benefits and reductions in personal income tax.

c) Investment

A.44 Though the construction industry's report specifically endorsed the Richardson Committee's conclusion that 'considerations other than taxation largely determine investment decisions', it was in their judgement on the long term effects on investment of a substitution of a VAT for part of the corporation tax, that the EDCs differed most in their emphasis from the Richardson Committee. Some replies (Chemicals, Clothing, Mechanical Engineering, Food, Electronics, Motor Manufacturing, the SMMT Panel and the BEAMA Taxation Panel) specifically mentioned that the greater use, in the years since the Richardson Committee reported, of more sophisticated techniques of appraising investment meant that companies were nowadays more sensitive than they had been to changes in the after-tax rates of return on investment. This was especially true of the more progressive companies who also tend to be industry price leaders (Mechanical Engineering EDC). The SMMT Panel spelt out how this (and greater corporate liquidity as a result of the cut in corporation tax) would in due course lead to more investment and lower prices, and so strengthen the competitive position of its industry.

A.45 The Motor Manufacturing EDC, while concurring that in the long run prices would be lower if corporation tax were reduced, added that a small reduction of (say) 5 percentage points in corporation tax was more likely to lead to a reappraisal of investment plans than to an immediate adjustment in prices. A statement by the Rubber EDC was in the same spirit '... in the long run a reduction in corporation tax might lead to a fall in prices ... in the short run businesses would not have sufficient confidence in the permanence of the reduction to reduce prices'. The Chemicals EDC thought, in recognising that estimates of the after-tax rate of return on investment is not always decisive in deciding on the investment, that a 5 per cent cut in corporation tax would not be sufficient to make an impact. If the cut were 10 per cent, *and* if companies could be persuaded that it was permanent, some chemical companies might *anticipate* the price reductions which the greater investment would bring in the long run. All the same, it doubted whether its industry needed any additional stimulus to invest. So long as prices were unchanged (and rent and rates could be set off against liability to VAT), the Hotel and Catering EDC thought that its industry's profitability, or at least the hotel section of it, would be slightly enhanced by the substitution of the VAT for part of the corporation tax, but that this would not stimulate investment unless the substitution were a sizeable one—at least a cut of 5 percentage points in the corporation tax.

A.46 The Oil Industry Taxation Committee commented that its industry was already very capital-intensive (with fixed assets at about £5,000 per man) and further capital substitution was unlikely to result from a VAT. However, provided full credits for VAT on capital equipment purchases were granted, the industry considered that a VAT would be advantageous to a firm with a higher ratio of capital to labour than its competitors and it would expect to derive competitive benefits from this.

A.47 It was, however, not unanimously thought that the tax change would be of great significance. In the distributive trades, the effect 'would be slight and would operate only in the long term'. It might be '... useful ... but many other factors bear on investment decisions' (Rubber EDC). 'The most important stimulus to a company's investment ... is confidence in the future demand for its products ... and the need to maintain its competitive position'. The view of the Distributive Trades EDC was that the stimulus of the tax change to investment in its own industry would be small, because after-tax profitability is only one consideration in investment appraisal and 'the scope for mechanisation is limited'. 'Direct investment incentives ... are the only really effective inducement to invest.' The Wool Textiles EDC was in agreement with this last opinion: 'Re-equipment in industry is more ... effectively promoted ... by a higher rate of investment grant.' The Motor Vehicle Distribution and Repair EDC also drew attention to the benefits its industry would derive if tax allowances were available on its workshop buildings.

A.48 The BEAMA Taxation Panel, too, thought that the tax change would not be a major stimulus. It would perhaps help a little by increasing liquidity. Two of the thirteen chairmen of the electrical engineering companies who wrote to the chairman of their industry's EDC thought the stimulus would be 'definite'; four of 'some positive effect'. None, however, thought it would be negative. The Printing and Publishing report concluded that the tax changes would be of little or no importance to the newspaper industry or to publishers, and the lack of 'labour flexibility' in the printing industry would constrict its impact on mechanisation there. The Paper and Board EDC as a body recognised that the tax change might theoretically stimulate more mechanisation, but could not agree whether it would do so in their own industry which is already highly capital intensive.

A.49 The Post Office EDC made the point that investment in postal and telecommunication services was 'demand led', though currently limited by the shortage of capacity in the supply industry. If demand for its industry's services fell as a consequence of the increased charges which the tax change might bring (depending on the form of the VAT for the Post Office), the extensive investment programmes now planned might be 'inhibited'. The Agriculture EDC did not believe that the forces now making for the rapid mechanisation of its industry would be strengthened by the tax change. Clothing, another EDC with many unincorporated businesses in its industry, thought that the tax change would *curtail* the investment of the smaller firms. The funds available to such firms for investment would be cut back by the need to finance stocks at the new tax-inclusive prices. To the larger companies the tax change 'would not do any positive harm' except with regard to administrative costs.

d) An export incentive?

A.50 The Food Manufacturing, Distributive Trades and Agriculture reports made the point that exports were of little concern to their industries. The same is true of the newspaper industry and printing (Printing and Publishing EDC). The Food Manufacturing EDC added, however, that it thought the substitution of an indirect tax which was rebateable on exports, for a direct tax which was not, should be helpful to exports, though, since it regarded a reduction in corporation tax as highly unlikely, the EDC had in mind here the personal income tax rather than the corporation tax.

A.51 Commonly, the EDCs expressed fears that the lower prices of exports which the substitution of a VAT for the corporation tax might bring would be quickly eroded by the sharp upward thrust which the tax change would give to the wage-price spiral. If this erosion (and the following observations were strongly subjected to this qualification) could be avoided, there was some optimism. The BEAMA Taxation Panel thought that 'some marginal benefits might emerge after a time' if its industry's suppliers did not increase their tax-exclusive prices. About half of the thirteen industrialists who wrote to the chairman of the Electrical Engineering EDC thought that they might be able to reduce prices, though the others saw no such possibility. The SMMT Panel were reasonably confident that their manufacturers' exports would benefit. Some small advantages seemed possible to the Mechanical Engineering, Clothing and Rubber EDCs, and the Wool Textiles EDC at least so far as 'wool tops, noils and wastes' were concerned. The Electronics EDC took a contrary view to the BEAMA Taxation Panel, and foresaw 'more than a marginal advantage'. Publishers thought they would be assisted in granting 'the larger discounts which were expected by overseas customers', but added that there were probably far less complicated ways of achieving this, eg the old export rebate scheme.

A.52 A number of EDCs stressed the limited importance of small price reductions in capturing export markets: quality, individuality, variety and prompt delivery were more essential to success in exporting, and in the case of wool cloth, for example, in some markets quota restrictions were decisive. Mechanical engineering products, too, 'depend as much on qualities of design, delivery and after-sales service' as on small price changes.

A.53 The conspicuous exception to this (highly qualified) optimism was the Chemicals EDC. Not only did it see the 'distinct risk' that the chemicals industry would be 'worse off' than at present, it believed the industry could not 'profitably expand exports much faster than it is doing unless its major market, ie the home economy, was also growing at a significantly higher rate than in the past or unless we had gained entry to some wider trading area such as the EEC'. 'By itself a VAT does nothing to help exports. The rebate merely removes the tax which has been placed on home consumption of the product.'

A.54 The Hotel and Catering EDC made the point that over half the expenditure of overseas visitors is on the services of hotels and restaurants. Whether the tax change could stimulate these 'invisible exports' would depend on whether the taxed inputs could be precisely identified. The Board of Trade has argued in the past that under present tax arrangements they cannot be identified with sufficient precision to secure tax exemption.

e) An import–saving incentive?

A.55 As with its effect on exports, the effect on imports of the substitution of the VAT for part of the corporation tax depends mainly on the consequences of the tax change for home prices. Fears were again common amongst the EDCs that the consequences would be so inflationary as to more than eliminate any possible discouragement to imports. In this event imports would finish more price-competitive than before.

A.56 Even on the assumption that price changes were not unfavourable, the EDCs were on the whole pessimistic that the tax change would lead to significant import-saving. The most definite exception was perhaps the Paper and Board EDC. The rubber industry, which depends on imports for a large percentage of its raw materials, would be unlikely to cut back the volume of these essential supplies.

A.57 The BEAMA Panel, which also observed that some sectors of the electrical industry import a 'fairly large' proportion of their raw materials, doubted whether there would be 'any significant effect' on imports, though on this, as on exports, the Electronics EDC held a more optimistic view. The consensus amongst the thirteen industrialists in electrical engineering went in favour of the Panel. The Panel's view on imports of capital goods was that quality and availability are the determining factors. It did, however, add that overseas suppliers of consumer durables would probably 'absorb' a large part of the VAT so far as the tax was an additional tariff. (This would lead to a lower import bill in terms of foreign exchange.)

A.58 The Mechanical Engineering EDC thought that 'at best' the effect on imports would be small because the volume of its industry's imports was 'relatively insensitive to marginal changes in price'. The Food Manufacturing EDC thought that the tax change would be no inducement to import-saving while the SMMT Panel thought that it would be. The Printing and Publishing EDC reported that the newspaper industry's requirements of imported wood pulp would not be cut significantly because home supplies cannot be much increased. The industry's imports of equipment depend 'not on price but on technical excellence and availability'. Printers and publishers foresaw only marginal advantages. The oil industry did not envisage that the balance of exports and imports of fuel would be much affected by the substitution of VAT for part of corporation tax. The international scope of the industry's operations made geographical, technical and political factors prevail over tax considerations.

A.59 As already mentioned, the Agriculture EDC foresaw that the overseas suppliers of many agricultural products would 'absorb' the VAT to a large extent and the Wool Textiles EDC, whose industry's main raw material is imported, thought there might be some substitution of synthetic products for wool, a substitution which it did not welcome and which would probably prejudice its export sales. Little reduction in the imports of cloth was to be expected.

A.60 An observation by the Chemicals EDC suggested that, if the tax change were made, the Prices and Incomes Board would have a role to play in offsetting the conflict between private and the country's economic interests. 'British producers of industrial chemicals would not be likely to reduce home prices in order to displace imports, even if they felt they had something in hand as a result of lower corporation tax, because this would usually mean reducing prices to their whole UK markets in order to gain a small increase in volume, and even then there would be no certainty that importers would not match the price cut.'

A.61 The EDCs had less to say on whether a substitution of the VAT for part of
the corporation tax would encourage businessmen to be more efficient in
saving labour and cutting costs generally. The printers' and publishers'
representatives drew attention to the relevance here of the administrative
costs of the VAT itself, particularly for the small businesses in their industry.
The Paper and Board EDC thought these increased administrative costs
might outweigh any gains from the greater efficiency the tax change should
stimulate.

A.62 The Hotel and Catering EDC made the same point as it had in relation to
investment: efficiency would be stimulated if there was a sizeable reduction
in corporation tax, but a commonly expressed view in the industry was that
the SET had, for the time being, induced as much labour-saving as any tax
can. The Distributive Trades EDC thought that the tax change must *in the
long run* benefit the more profitable businesses, though again it had in mind
chiefly the possibility of reductions in personal income tax rather than
corporation tax.

A.63 The Chemicals EDC accepted the Richardson Committee's view:
international competition and regular wage increases at home keep up a
continuous pressure to improve efficiency. Similarly, to the Motor Vehicles
Distribution and Repairs EDC high wages are the important incentive to
save labour: the tax change would not be 'of much significance'. In the
newspaper industry the intense competition which exists was enough to
increase efficiency. Publishers of books also had a 'reasonably good standard
of efficiency already'. They could cut costs by cutting stocks of books, but
this would lower the quality of the services they provided. The printers
again mentioned the constraint of labour inflexibility. In the construction
industries, VAT as a substitute for corporation tax might encourage labour-
saving, but not more than SET does. The general view that the search for
efficiency is—at present—as sharp as it can be was expressed by the Paper
and Board EDC at least in relation to the larger companies in its industry.
The Mechanical Engineering EDC took a rather contrary view: the lowering
of the tax liability of high margin companies relative to the liability of low
margin companies could have an effect on efficiency of some significance.

A.64 The Wool Textiles and Clothing EDCs presented rather more complex
cases. There is a wide range of profitability amongst firms in the wool
industry, and the tax change would probably favour the manufacturers of
man-made fibres. However, in some labour intensive sections of the industry,
for example the high class end of the mending trade, cost saving would be
achieved by lowering quality. The Clothing EDC feared that the rate of
return on capital in its industry would be so depressed by the tax change
that, although some labour saving would be stimulated, a more important
result might be a reduction in size of the industry and an increase in low
cost imports. The Oil Industry Taxation Committee considered that a tax

like VAT which was levied on value added, rather than on profits, was likely to encourage and benefit efficient firms.

A.65 Finally, it is notable that although the possibility that a VAT might be thought of as an alternative to an *increase* in corporation tax was referred to in the NEDO questionnaire, none of the EDCs sought to compare the effects upon prices, investment, exports or efficiency of an *uncompensated* VAT on the one hand, and an equal yield *increase* in corporation tax on the other.

The VAT as an extension of the base of indirect taxation

A.66 The attention of the EDCs was drawn to the fact that the possible economic benefits which might flow from substituting a VAT for part of the corporation tax, or from imposing a VAT rather than increasing the rate of corporation tax, depend on the reduced rate of corporation tax rather than the imposition of the substitute VAT. The substitute tax could equally well be the purchase tax, increased in rates and/or in coverage. The EDCs were asked to give their views on the VAT as an extension of the base of indirect taxation, both in general terms and, more especially, from the point of view of their own particular industries.

A.67 While the various sections of the Printing and Publishing EDC saw nothing but disadvantages for their industries in the substitution of a VAT for the purchase tax, some printers thought that 'the structure of indirect taxation was . . . long overdue for reform . . . the replacement of this by a universal low rate VAT would be regarded as more beneficial to industry . . .' The Paper and Board EDC saw the substitution as 'detrimental' to its industry.

A.68 The Distributive Trades EDC made the point that to extend indirect taxation more or less comprehensively as would be done by a VAT is essentially a political decision. The Chemicals EDC would leave a decision on the VAT till entry into the EEC is assured. Meanwhile, it believes that all the changes in the tax structure which it thinks desirable (broadly a significant shift from direct to indirect taxation) could be made without introducing a VAT. The construction industry said that, since half the output of the industry consists of capital works, any type of sales or purchase tax which impinged only on sales to consumers (in this instance housing) would free the construction industry from a considerable administrative burden.

A.69 The Rubber EDC also favoured the purchase tax as against the VAT on grounds of administrative cost, although it thought the VAT inevitable 'for EEC reasons'. It was not, however, unconcerned about how any possible change in the purchase tax was effected. It was 'entirely opposed' to simply increasing the rates, with the increased discrimination which this was likely to entail against its main customers the manufacturers of motor cars and of domestic appliances. Other criticisms of the 'selectivity' aspect of the purchase tax were expressed not only because of the arbitrary element in the discrimination (Clothing, Food Manufacturing EDCs and the SMMT Taxation Panel), but also because in practice it involved sharp changes in the rates from time to time (Chemicals EDC). A more widely based consumption tax like the VAT at a low uniform rate (or at least at a few rates with a much lower spread than the purchase tax) would not only be an improvement in the structure of indirect taxation (Food Manufacturing EDC) but could provide a 'better regulator . . . in that regulatory changes in the rates could avoid a special impact on some goods' (Electrical Engineering EDC). The SMMT Panel also fear that if the coverage of the purchase tax were extended the tax's spill over on to industrial costs might be so great as to justify the extra administrative costs of the VAT to avoid it. At the same time the Panel recognised that if the VAT were levied at several different rates, the higher rates might continue to be used for regulatory purposes. The Wool Textiles EDC, while it saw no great advantages in the VAT as compared with the purchase tax, extended in rates or coverage, was in favour of a single rate for the VAT if it were to be introduced. This would be administratively cheaper and avoid arbitrariness. The EDC added that the higher rates of purchase tax could be retained for purposes of 'selectivity'.

A.70 The BEAMA and SMMT Taxation Panels commented on the advantages for their industries of a more uniform rate of tax on consumption. In the long run an increase in the volume of home sales of electrical appliances, TV sets, etc would assist the electrical engineering and electronics industries to reduce costs and help its exports. The SMMT Panel also advanced its frequently reiterated argument of a 'strengthened home base'. In line with this the Motor Vehicle Distribution and Repair EDC foresaw an increase in demand for garage services, though the EDC's welcome for the VAT carried a condition of payment arrangements 'comparable' to the present ones for purchase tax.

A.71 The Mechanical Engineering, Post Office, Clothing, Agriculture and Food Manufacturing EDCs all made the point that their industries would be likely to be less affected by an extended purchase tax than by a VAT. The 3–4 per cent VAT necessary to replace the revenue from purchase tax would mean that the Post Office would have to increase its postal charges by 2·2 per cent and its telecommunication charges by 0·9 per cent to regain the pre-VAT situation—in relation to net assets—even on the most favourable assumption that the tax-exclusive prices of the goods and services which the Post Office purchases were unchanged.

A.72 The Clothing EDC thought that the effect on its industry of a VAT as compared with a revised purchase tax, though 'difficult to assess' would generally be 'adverse', particularly if the high rates on clothing in 'some EEC countries' were applied. The manufacturers of children's clothing which does not now attract tax would suffer 'disproportionately'. This EDC was

opposed to the VAT solely as a substitute for the purchase tax, though if the VAT were introduced 'many members felt that it should extend to all goods . . . without discrimination'. (The plea of several EDCs for an investigation of the social consequences of a VAT may be recalled in this connection.) Though the Food Manufacturing EDC recognised that the products of its industry would probably fall under a VAT much more than under an extended purchase tax it expressed preferences (already noted above) for the VAT with minimum differentials in its rates 'because it would be less arbitrary, cause less distortion, would be less inequitable and would encourage and facilitate industrial planning by its greater stability'.
The Oil Industry Taxation Committee considered that a tax system incorporating lower specific duties and a VAT was capable of being more neutral than the present system and would be preferred by them.

A.73 The EDCs' comments on how the substitution of a VAT for the purchase tax would affect the *nature* of businessmen's pricing, investment, exporting and importing decisions were in broad agreement with the Richardson Committee's conclusion that its nature would be unchanged: the VAT, like the purchase tax, would be viewed as an indirect tax.

The VAT and the A.74 The EDCs were asked whether they saw any advantages or disadvantages
selective employment tax in a VAT (which included services) compared with the SET, having regard to the longer term effects on productivity which are claimed for the SET.

A.75 Many EDCs regard the SET as a bad tax, some very positively. The Distributive Trades EDC was unanimous in its opposition to the tax as 'discriminatory, anomalous, and distorting of economic processes'. The SMMT Panel thought the SET clumsy—not only in its application as between services and manufacturing, and because it doubts the tax's contribution to long term productivity, but also because it falls on export services 'like insurance, wharfage, packing and delivery'. It looks forward to the results of the Reddaway enquiry into the SET which may throw light on the spill-over of the tax on to manufacturing costs which it believes 'must be significant'.

A.76 The BEAMA Panel judged 'doubtful' the SET's effects on productivity and thought the tax should be abolished. The SMMT Panel did not think a VAT would be worthwhile simply to replace the SET. Though manufacturers of food products almost certainly pay less under the SET than they would pay under a VAT, the industry's EDC thought that the SET leads to 'gross anomalies in the siting of offices, computers, warehouses, and decisions on staffing'. The Wool Textiles EDC thought the SET was 'discriminatory, costly to administer, and ineffective in transferring labour'. It falls on a 'substantial number' of merchants exporting wool products. To the Rubber EDC it was a 'bad anomalous tax . . . ' and ' . . . less likely than the VAT to stimulate efficiency'. To the Motor Vehicle Distribution and Repair EDC the tax's distorting effects on the economy were 'undesirable'.

A.77 Hotels and restaurants are amongst the businesses which have particularly felt the burden of the SET. They have met it, as their EDC's report states, by a combination of price increases and cost economies: 'Cooper Brothers found that firms . . . have assimilated the effects of SET of 1½ per cent in suppliers' prices'. The EDC concluded that the substitution of a uniform VAT for the SET (and the purchase tax)' . . . would have favourable effects on the industry', though little effect on prices.

A.78 The Chemicals EDC was critical of the SET, though less positively than some others. It thought a VAT 'preferable' because 'less liable to distort'. The Printing and Publishing EDC reported no advantages for their industries in a substitution of an equal-yield VAT for the SET (the Government has promised publishers exemption from the SET 'at the first opportunity') but the printers were disposed to think that the tax change might be generally beneficial to the British economy.

A.79 The attitudes of six other EDCs were contrasting. The Mechanical Engineering EDC found a possible substitution of a VAT for the SET 'not attractive'. As far as its industry was concerned it would be to substitute a tax for a loan to the Government outside the development areas and a tax for a subsidy in the development areas. The Paper and Board EDC also saw 'no advantages'. The Post Office provided estimates of the increased postal and telecommunications charges that would be necessary if the present SET were replaced by a 1 per cent VAT (0·7 per cent on postal and 0·3 per cent on telecommunications). The judgment of the Clothing EDC was that 'the substitution . . . for the SET in its present form would be disadvantageous to the industry . . . probably', while the Hosiery and Knitwear EDC expressed concern about the danger of losing the regional incentives especially in the development areas if the SET was abolished. Similarly, there would be no advantages to agriculture from the switch (Agriculture EDC).

A.80 The construction industries' joint report referred to the strong opposition which exists in the industry to the SET especially to its discriminatory aspect, 'but it does not oppose a payroll tax as such, and to the extent that any tax on labour acts as an incentive to greater productivity (which many sections of the industry deny) it is believed that SET is more effective than a VAT'. The administrative costs of this existing tax are also much lower than those which a VAT would impose on the industry.

A.81 The Distributive Trades EDC saw no difference in the effects of the SET and VAT on pricing policies, both 'will tend to be passed on . . . as a direct cost'. If anything, the VAT was 'more certain in its passing on'. The Motor Vehicle Distribution and Repair EDC reckoned that a 5 per cent VAT would have the same effect on its industry prices as the SET at £1.37½ per male worker. It did, however, express some doubt whether the abolition of the SET would be taken into account in prices, unless positive efforts were made in that direction '. . . it would be a complicated task to identify and nullify such price increases'. The construction paper contained similar doubts. The oil industry was little affected by SET, but did not regard a substitution of VAT as disadvantageous, so long as there were some compensating reductions in the existing oil duties.

The VAT as a benefit to capital-intensive methods of production

A.82 Under certain assumptions, chiefly a rise in labour costs greater than the tax-exclusive prices of capital equipment (the VAT element in the cost of the equipment is, of course, rebatable), a VAT would benefit firms whose capital costs are high in relation to their labour costs as compared with firms in the reverse position, quite apart from whether taxes on profits have been simultaneously reduced.

A.83 The EDCs were asked to comment on how varied 'capital-labour ratios' are in their industries and thus on the scope for this process to work with an indication as to how rapidly mechanisation would be stimulated if it did work. There were differences of opinion as to how a change in the relative prices of labour and capital would affect mechanisation. The BEAMA Taxation Panel thought it unlikely to provide a significant additional incentive. (Wages already are a powerful labour-saving incentive and companies already invest in the most up-to-date equipment). The SMMT Taxation Committee, on the other hand, thought that in the long run it would lead to some increase in the capital intensity of methods of production, and this view was shared by some representatives on the Printing and Publishing EDC, though the scope in their own industries was limited as, to take another report, it was in the paper and board industry.

A.84 In the mechanical engineering and wool industries capital-labour ratios vary considerably, in the experience of the industries' EDCs, amongst firms which are earning comparable rates of return on the capital they employ. The Mechanical Engineering EDC was not able to assess how speedily the more capital-intensive firms would respond with even more mechanisation to a change which favoured them against their less capital-intensive competitors. In the Wool Textiles EDC's opinion there are more effective ways of stimulating mechanisation.

A.85 The main contrast in motor manufacturing (according to the SMMT Panel) is not between competitive but between complementary sectors of the industry, namely between the vehicle manufacturers on the one hand and the distributors and the manufacturers of accessories on the other. The Motor Vehicle Distribution and Repair EDC stated that there were no wide variations in capital-intensity between garages 'or likely to be in the future'. Similarly, the Chemicals EDC stated that there were not many important examples of disparity in capital-intensity between firms making the same product. In agriculture also, as the industry's EDC established from a study of farm accounts, the contrast is much greater between farmers in different sectors of the industry than between farmers in the same sector. The industry's EDC added '... there can be no question of assuming that in agriculture labour-intensive enterprises are necessarily wasteful users of manpower ... We are anxious again to refute any suggestion that steps need to be taken to speed up the outflow of labour from the industry above the present substantial rate ... indeed we believe that measures may have to be taken to slow it down.' In construction, mechanisation 'is relatively unimportant compared with the need for better organisation and site management'.

Printed in England for Her Majesty's Stationery Office by
Williams Lea/WLP Group/London
Dd 500805 K40 4/71